# GIVE THANKS

## WITH A
## GRATEFUL HEART

CHRIS THOMAS

Dedication

In memory of my aunty Maureen
who learned the wisdom of gratitude
in her long life and who, because of that,
loved every moment of her ninety-four years.

Thankyou!

# GIVE THANKS
## WITH A GRATEFUL HEART

First published in 2018 by
New Life Publishing, Luton,
Bedfordshire LU4 9HG

British Library Cataloguing in Publication Data
A catalogue record for this book is available
from the British Library


ISBN   978 1 912237 11 1

Unless otherwise stated Bible references are
from the New Jerusalem Bible, Darton, Longman
and Todd, UK (1985) and are used with permission.

Typesetting by New Life Publishing,
Luton, UK   www.goodnewsbooks.co.uk
Printed and bound in Great Britain

# CONTENTS

# FOREWORD

Liverpool in the 1960's was an exciting place to be, but it was also a place of great poverty and struggle, and I suppose my early life could be summed up in those two words. My family was poor, living in the upstairs of a semi-detached house and sharing the toilet with the patients of a doctor's surgery housed below; and we struggled. We were poor because my Dad was alcoholic and, as a result of that, we struggled to hold things together as a family despite my mum's best efforts.

The early childhood experiences I had scarred me badly, and gratitude for anything was very much on the back burner. Despite my experience of coming alive in God and my awareness that I was loved by God and, more than that, God was in love with me, I found it very difficult to be grateful. Everything in my life was tinged with sadness. I have described it in other places as 'low level depression'. When I broke down because I could not cope with all that I had buried from my past, things eventually became a lot better, but my glass was still, usually, only half full.

Having said that, I have always been aware, since my encounter with God, that gratitude is key to the Christian life. Early on in my journey, I heard in many places the call to praise God in the midst of every situation and I wondered how I could do that. It seemed too hard. I knew I wanted to be more grateful. I wanted to be grateful for love, for friendship, for God, for humanity and for the world. So, I decided, after various experiences and encounters, to cultivate gratitude. I guess that really is the journey that I am on; trying to be grateful and still, at times, wrestling with those inner demons that would choke gratitude. One of the things I do is to make it my business every morning to name ten things that I have to be grateful for. I find that it is extraordinary how  doing that lifts and changes my mood. Another thing I do is never to leave a shop or restaurant without saying thank you to those who have served me, whatever the quality of service! Little things that build up the store of gratitude within.

I quote often in the book from people like Richard Rohr and Ronald Rolheiser and others who have discovered that gratitude is key to transforming both ourselves, others, and this beautiful fragile world that we live in. Indeed, it is Rolheiser who understands that the only heart that can transform the world is the grateful heart. I am still trying to learn that.

This book has been written to help others who, like me, struggle with being grateful. It has been written to remind all of us that we have much to be grateful for in our lives and it is a reflection on the truth that does not depend on our feelings; the truth that God is good and that gratitude should become our default setting.

# ONE

# GIVE THANKS FOR THE GOODNESS OF GOD

I n 1976 I went to my first Prayer group and was warmly welcomed into that prayer community by a man called Denis. I was a shy retiring sixteen year old with all the baggage that comes from an alcoholic father. He was a blunt Yorkshire man who with his friend Teresa had been walking in the ways of love for many years. He exuded kindness and compassion, all because of his unshakeable belief in the goodness of God.

I had experienced a huge encounter with God which Denis had been part of and it seemed to be his mandate to keep an eye on me. He wanted to make sure that I grew in my relationship with God. He and Teresa became hugely important in my formative years as they encouraged me to pray, to read the Scriptures and study them and to believe in my own giftedness.

Denis was always laughing. Even when his life was tough, which it often was, he smiled and laughed and thanked God. I learnt from him what it meant to say that God is good even in the worst of times. I learnt from him that the goodness of God was not dependent on the circumstances of my life, that God is simply good.

Many years after Denis had died I met Mike Stanley, the

co-founder of CJM music. Mike would often begin their times
of ministry by calling into the microphone 'God is good' and the
people would respond 'all the time.' Then Mike would say 'and
all the time' and the people in front of him would respond 'God
is good'. Mike lived out that truth until the day he died at the
very young age of forty eight.

Of course that belief in the goodness of God gives rise to many
questions. How is it possible to say that God is good when the
world is full of suffering and pain? How do you say God is good
when you look at what has happened in Syria? Can God be good
when we look at the children, victims of war, who have been
damaged physically and emotionally, traumatised by the violence
that they have seen? How is it possible to say that God is good
when your loved ones die tragically? Is it possible to say that God
is good when you have been abused and damaged so badly by
humanity that you can hardly function? Many would argue that
it is not possible; that God, if God exists, is not good. Rather, it
is argued that God, if God exists, is capricious, evil and vengeful
and that humanity is on the receiving end of God's malevolence.
I find that attitude extremely easy to understand if one has not
had an experience of, or an encounter with, the reality of God.
Without entering into the mystery and opening ourselves to the
mystery, it is easy to believe that we are simply pawns in the
hands of some sort of megalomaniac.

So where do we go to reflect on the goodness of God in a world
torn apart? I would always say go to the Scriptures, but please
do not leave your brain behind you when you start to reflect and

pray. The Scriptures are the faith story of a people growing in awareness of God. If you read them literally, then God is indeed at times petty and vengeful; as you read stories of God's engagement with the enemies of the people of Israel. It seems that many are destroyed by God. God appears to be partisan and selective in the bestowing of love and the bestowing of vengeance. However, if you read the Scriptures taking on board the scholarship and reflection of many people throughout history, you begin to see a different truth emerging.

In order to discover that truth of a God who woos and beckons and loves, we have to spend time reflecting, and over the years I have reflected on the Scriptures I have become more and more aware of just how powerful they are and the effect they can have on our lives as we discover a God who is anything but violent and vengeful.

Elizabeth was a woman from County Down who I met when I first started going to prayer groups in the 1970's. She was a lovely woman always full of fun and laughter and constantly thanking God for everything in her life. The prayer group were putting on a series of talks called The Life in the Spirit Seminars and Elizabeth was asked to give the talk on growth. She stood up and began to give her testimony. It was a really sad story. She had been orphaned at the age of three when her parents were killed in a train crash. Her family were very poor and none of her aunts or uncles could look after Elizabeth and her five siblings. The children were all split up and put into various orphanages. They missed each other terribly. Elizabeth said that she was never abused by the sisters she was placed with but nor was she shown much compassion or love. Her every material need was met. She was warm, fed and clothed but never loved. She said that she left the place when she was sixteen emotionally stunted with a poor self-image, thinking that she was unlovable. Her life of faith had been stunted too. She had been fed an image of God that terrified her. She went to Mass because she believed that if she did not go then hell would be her reward. Whatever she did was never enough because God was cruel and demanding.

She said that she was at Church one Sunday morning. It was just after Vatican II and her Parish Priest was very excited by all that the Council promised. He advertised a scripture group as starting the week after and Elizabeth said she went, not knowing why, but drawn towards it. From the first meeting Elizabeth loved it. The weeks went by and grew into months and Elizabeth's understanding of God slowly began to change. As she prayed and reflected on the Scriptures she discovered that God is good. As she discovered that, her image of herself began to change and she found her poor self-image began to be healed and she grew in self-confidence. It was a marvellous testimony to growth, change and a new awareness of the goodness of God

So what do the Scriptures tell us about God? I think that primarily it is that God is good because God is love. Throughout the Old or First Testament we read the story of a people who are growing in awareness of who God is. What we can discover is that God is a God of abundance and creativity who is on the side of those in need. We find that God is a God very much identified with the human situation, that God is with his people. Jeremiah and Ezekiel, in the middle of the trauma of exile and displacement, can still say that God will not abandon Israel because God is good.

I really believe that is the truth the Scriptures are telling us. Often that truth lies behind the stories and the images used, and the Spirit wants to reveal that truth to us. It is at that level the Scriptures are inspired. The Scriptures will enable us to discover who God is if we give them the space and the time.

At the beginning of the Bible we are reminded that everything God creates is good. Everything is created out of love and that love is imaginative and ingenious. It is pure energy and power. Everything we know that exists, the universe, the world, every living creature is a result of this extraordinary energy and power taking shape and form. That of course includes you and me. In whatever way you were conceived, you were wanted from the very moment of creation by a God whose love is at the very core of your being. You have a dignity that no-one and nothing can take away from you. That is why as Church we have to be against anything that erodes human dignity.

One of the greatest gifts I have been given in the last twenty years is to encounter some amazing people. One of them is Sister Helen Prejean, the nun whose story was told in the film *Dead Man Walking*. Helen came to Newcastle to speak at a conference and I was lucky enough to have dinner with her. The next day I asked her if she would be willing to come to Liverpool and she said she would. Helen was due back in Newcastle to speak again the next year and it was arranged that Helen would leave Newcastle and drive with me to Liverpool where she would address a group of people. The year after came very quickly and I found myself in the car with Helen. She had just spoken at the Newcastle conference and I presumed she would be exhausted. Not at all! She got into the car, and her first question in her broad Louisiana accent was, 'Got any Beatles songs?' Thank God I had, because for the next three hours Helen sang every Beatle song you can imagine at the top of her voice. She spent the next two days with us and then the year after she came back. Every time I met this wonderful woman of God I was moved by the sense of dignity she had for humanity, particularly for the poor and the broken. Every moment of her life is spent upholding the dignity of the human person from birth to natural death. She tells heart-rending stories about people on death row whose dignity is taken from them as they wait for the inevitable. I will forever thank God for this woman who knows that God is good and who loves every vestige of humanity because of that. As I have listened to her I am always reminded of the dignity and wonder of the human person.

As we read what we call the historical books, the stories of the founding of a nation and kings whose names are virtually unpronounceable, we are invited to discover a God who is desperately in love with us but who meets us where we are, gently leading us towards the full revelation of love in Jesus.

It would be ridiculous to say that it is the only image of God that we are given in these books. As I have already said there are battles, prayers and lots of unsolicited violence in the historical books that make God look like a vile petty dictator. I think the truth is that God took the people of Israel where they were with their particular moral understanding and development. They could not conceive of a God that was anything other than the Gods they understood from other nations who were all violent and punishing. Indeed, in their misunderstanding, any God who was not violent and partisan was not worthy of the name. So God took them where they were and gently tried to move them on, tried to show them the truth and power of the love that God had for them.

There are times when they almost get it, particularly in books like the Song of Songs, that beautiful Hebrew love story. A few years ago I led a short course on the Song of Songs, that wonderful earthy reflection on human love, sexuality and desire. Some of the Scholars that I read said that the mutual complementarity of the two lovers express something of the image of the relationship between God and humanity. God desires that same sort of intimacy with us, knowing and being known, mutual giving and unbridled love. It is amazing when we begin to sense it and it leads more fully into they mystery of the goodness of God.

Some of the Prophets also illustrate that goodness and love, like Hosea's beautiful story about the unfaithful wife and the love that constantly takes her back. You find it in Ezekiel's wonderful vision of the valley of dry bones that God breathes into and raises

to life. It is there in Jeremiah's growing understanding that God
wants to create a new covenant of love with God's people and it
is wonderful to read. There really are times when those early
writers almost grasp what is impenetrable.

As I have said, it is also true that there are times when they lose
that sense of God altogether and cry out to God to destroy their
enemies. It is then that they see in their own violence and
threatening behaviour, which was part of the culture of the day,
the hand of God. Did God really wreak vengeance on Israel's
enemies? Of course not but that was their interpretation of what
happened. The story never changes. Sometimes we glimpse the
overwhelming gift of love and benevolence and at other times we
lose it completely. It seems to me that often we human beings
create God in our own image and likeness and make God into a
more self-righteous version of ourselves. Yet, when we glimpse it
we know the truth that God is good and all we can say is thank
you.

One of my mum's best friends was lady called Teresa. As I have
written before, in other books, Teresa's simple, some might say
blind, faith was a huge inspiration to me. I would often see her
in the middle of conversations, cross herself, raise her eyes to
heaven and silently mouth 'thank you'. That it was a bit like a
Les Dawson sketch, does not seem to matter now. At the time it
seemed to a youngster like me a bit twee and overly zealous.
However the image has remained with me and what did matter
was that Teresa unconsciously was witnessing to a God that was
good. Thanksgiving punctuated her life even when times were

hard and for her, and times had been very hard, but God was still good.

Our Christian understanding of God as a Trinity of persons is all about mutuality, abiding love and goodness. The early North African Church Father, Augustine, used the illustration of two lovers, and the mutual love which binds them, in order to picture the relations of the persons of the Trinity.

As you reflect on the Trinity, you discover a trinity of persons totally giving everything for the sake of the other, and then receiving that same self-giving back from another. When I watched the film *The Shack* that mutual love was imaged very beautifully. The Trinity is a non-stop waterfall of love. Each person is totally and completely accepted by the other. God is perfect love, given and received and shared with humanity. So God can only be good.

The spiritual journey of recognising that mutual giving and receiving of love is a journey we all have to undertake in order to believe that God is good. Without an existential experience of this love that flows from the Trinity it takes most of our lives to realise that we are accepted and to learn to accept everyone else if we ever do realise it. Most of us cannot do this easily because deep inside ourselves there is so much self-accusation and poor self-esteem. Most of us are so convinced that we are not the body of Christ, that we are unworthy, that we are not in radical union with God that it blocks us from knowing the truth of God's goodness. If we do not know that we are connected intimately to God, then how can we ever say that God is good?

The truth is that the question of our union with God has already been resolved once and for all. We see it in the person of Christ, the face of God hanging on a tree, giving everything for us. It has existed since the beginning of time but in Christ we see it. We cannot create our union with God. It is objectively already given to us by the Holy Spirit who dwells within us and never ever abandons us. It was St Augustine who said, 'God loves each of us as if there were only one of us'. That is how extraordinary God's desire is for us.

I was recently in a local prison and met there a man in his forties. He was a long-term offender and was a drug addict who both sold and took drugs. His story was typical of many of the prisoners as he shared the inadequate parenting that he had received. His mother was a prostitute abandoned by her family; his father had long since disappeared. What chance did he have? At school he was declared a wastrel for whom nothing good would come. No-one saw his pain and heartache. He was simply trouble that had to be dealt with. He began to believe the lie that he was no good and gave up on himself. Things went from bad to worse. He left school, already with a string of petty crimes behind him, and it was only a matter of time before he was sucked into the drug scene. This led him into protection rackets and a life of violence. He told me that he was a hard man but that he ached inside himself to know love. He had a string of failed relationships behind him and it seemed as though there was no way forward.

Every Tuesday our team would go to the prison and share

something of the love of God. This man would sit staring at the floor. I watched as he began to respond to what he heard, so much so that by the end of the month his heart had been softened. He had begun to hear the good news of God's love for him. He began to read the Scriptures and to pray each day. He became aware of his own dignity and value. He discovered that God is good and it changed his life. I obviously do not know what the future holds for him and it would be naïve to think that everything in his garden was suddenly rosy. However at least for that time the process of transformation had begun within him and his experience could never be taken away from him.

When we begin to discover that God is good we begin to know that whenever we become aware of God's presence, God drops everything and gives us undivided attention. It is total attention from the most important person in our lives. Who could ask anything more of a human mother, or father? Who could ask anything more of God? Some while back I heard a song the chorus of which repeats, 'You're a good, good father. It's who you are. It's who you are and I'm loved by you.' If only we knew that truth in the depths of our hearts then we would give thanks because of the goodness of God. Thomas Merton, who was an American Catholic convert, writer, theologian and mystic, once said 'To be grateful is to recognise the Love of God in everything He has given us - and He has given us everything. Every breath we draw is a gift of His love, every moment of existence is a grace, for it brings with it immense graces from Him. Gratitude therefore takes nothing for granted, is never unresponsive, is constantly awakening to new wonder and to praise of the goodness of God. For the grateful person knows that God is good, not by hearsay but by experience. And that is what makes all the difference.'

Do you really know the truth that God desires you with all the desire of a lover for the beloved? Do you know that you are the apple of God's eye? Do you know that God is good?

The Scriptures want to take you to that place where you know it is true and all the suffering and the shame that dogs our hearts and minds can finally be put to rest as we let the essence of God fill our soul, our mind, our being. It is then that we can finally say with Augustine, 'Our hearts are restless until they rest in you O God'. God is indeed good and the circumstances of our lives do not change the goodness of God.

Some years ago when on retreat in Scotland I met a woman called Fran. We got talking one night and she shared with me her upbringing as a Catholic in Glasgow in the 1940's. She said it was beaten into her that God was good. She went to Mass faithfully more out of fear than anything else. When she was in her mid twenties she had an encounter with God on a beach. She had gone there to reflect on a breakdown in a relationship and it was while she was on that beach crying out to God that her very being, as she put it, was flooded with peace and love. She said that she returned to Glasgow a different woman. Fran met Mike, they married, settled down, had four children and then tragedy struck. Her husband was killed in a freak dockyard accident. She was beside herself and held on to life by her fingertips. She said despite that hardship she never doubted God was good and God was with her. She brought her children up and then, wonder of wonders, met Dave.

She did not think she would ever be as happy as she had been again, and with Dave it was different, but happiness was hers. They loved each other and he showed her more about faith and God's love and she said that she grew in love of God and life. A sudden heart attack took Dave and still Fran knew the truth that God is good. When I met her she was spending time in the retreat centre because her youngest daughter had taken her own life and she was trying to come to terms with it, if you ever can. Despite all the tragedy of her life still she never doubted the goodness of God. As she shared her painful story her own goodness and bravery shone through as well as her pain and confusion. All she knew, and what she was holding on to, was that the love that she had encountered on that beach had never let her down and she did not think that God would ever let her down. She knew that God would fill her with peace again because 'God is good.'

As I listened to her I was reminded of a quotation by Richard Rohr, the American Franciscan, who, reflecting on the prophet Jonah, said in one of his daily meditations, 'God's way of restoring things interiorly is much more patient and finally more effective. God lets Jonah run in the wrong direction, until this reluctant prophet finds a long, painful, circuitous path to get back where he needs to be - in spite of himself! Looking in your own 'rear-view mirror' can fill you with gratitude for God's work in your life.'

God is good and if we take time to reflect and pray and look at the Scriptures we will discover that goodness and know that it is always present sustaining us and guiding us. Take time to look back in your rear view mirror and see how good God is.

So give thanks for the goodness of God poured out upon us. Give thanks for the desire of God to be with us always. Give thanks with a heart full of gratitude that God is not distant and scary or capricious and nasty, as some would have us believe. Give thanks that God is good and has chosen to let the goodness overflow into this magnificent, wonderful world filled with wonder and awe. Give thanks!

# TWO

# GIVE THANKS FOR THE BEAUTY OF CREATION

Several years ago I went with a friend on holiday to South Africa. We stayed in Cape Town for a few days and then hired a car and began to drive along the garden route. As we drove we were surrounded by extraordinary scenery. We saw whales and dolphins frolicking in the sea. We watched colonies of penguins waddling around. It was the most glorious, wonderful invitation to rejoice in the wonder of creation and give thanks.

We finished off the holiday with a four-day safari. It was magnificent as we saw animals that we would never see, lions, hippos, white rhinos, cheetahs, giraffes all living in their own environment. I remember sitting on our jeep one day in complete silence as a pride of lions circled the vehicle. I was awe-struck as I gazed at these wonderful animals. I think our guide was relieved when they passed on without incident but oh! It was wonderful to see.

We crossed huge expanses of bush surrounded by mountains and watched magnificent sunsets and sunrises. One day at sunset we arrived at the top of a mountain where there was a wonderful vantage point looking out over the whole compound. Our guide opened the boot and pulled out a hamper and we toasted the creation with gin and tonic as the sun went down.

All I could do was give thanks for the beauty that was all around us. It was more than words can express and will live in my memory for ever and it created within me a sense of awe and wonder that has never really left me. The only disappointment is that we could not find the elephants on any of our excursions! How do you lose an elephant in the African bush?

Up to that point, and although I have seen many wonderful aspects of creation, I think I had rather taken it all for granted. I would miss the wonderful sunsets that we are given each day without noticing. I would take little note of the things around me, the animals and trees and plants. Now, however, after that experience I look at every tree and marvel. I look at clouds and skies and I am filled with amazement. I see the beauty in animals and in the created order and all I can do is give thanks.

This wonder has its roots in the Judeo Christian world view. That world view has it its basis in the  book of Genesis which is not a book of history. Nor is it a scientific account of the creation. It is not an eyewitness report of how the world and the human race began. It is an attempt to look at the relationship between God and creation and to know the truth that God is good, that creation is good, and for all of it we can give thanks.

These ancient stories reveal to us the face of God, a creative, wonderful God. Ronald Rolheiser, the Canadian oblate, says 'Should God's face speak more of maturity or raw energy, depth or colour, old age or youth, chastity or sex, creed or eroticism, obedience or creativity, tradition or novelty?'

How do we capture the reality of this God who, in our opening chapter, I tried to reveal as good and benevolent. The truth is we cannot capture God and put God in a box presuming we know and understand. As Rolheiser tries to imply, God is always more. For me the book of Genesis points us towards a God who will not be trapped, confined, caged or domesticated, a God in whom everything finds a place. We find a God that the prophets in our Scriptures began to understand. Obviously, they were contained by the society they lived in and the culture they came from but they glimpsed something bigger and more.

It seems to me that the purpose of the Scriptures is not to tell us ancient stories or to give us a list of do's and don'ts and moral hoops to jump through but to move us beyond ourselves into the mystery that is God.

That is why I love the prophets so much, because they are often pointing us beyond ourselves and indeed condemning much of our religious practice, which can be stultifying and dead ended, to a way of life that is rooted in intimacy with a God who wants to overwhelm us with the power of love. It is that 'overwhelming' that the Scriptures call us into.

Through ancient stories, epics, laws, songs, poems, dramas and myths, through characters that existed and some that never did, we are called beyond ourselves and into the realms of otherness. In the struggle of an ancient people to experience God we can see our own struggle. It is our story that these ancient writers tell if we open our eyes. You will find every struggle, heartache, emotion, question that you will ever have to face in the pages of these ancient books and it is all there to lead us into the mystery and wonder that is God. It is all there to fill us with thanksgiving.

Sadly most of us prefer unthreatening religion to the living God who breaks into our lives, shatters our understandings and turns us upside down. It is easier to go to Church and live by a particular moral code than to let God into our lives because when we do, that life will never again be ordered but it will be exciting. What the book of Genesis reveals is an exuberant God whose creativity cannot be contained and who is always surprising. I sometimes think that God scares us with the intensity of love and yet, if we are open, attracts us at the core of our being so that we are almost impelled to want the more.

Several years ago I was on retreat in a house of prayer and I met there a young man whose name was Mick. He was staying for a few days to try and, as he put it, get his head together. He told me that he was searching for God. His journey had led him away from the main line churches because he said, as he perceived it, we were too narrow. I remember him telling me that God was bigger and more than we could ever imagine and that no religion could ever say that it had the truth. We went for a walk one day down on the beach and as we walked, he talked of his desire for a God that scared the pants off him. He talked and talked of his search for God and how that search had led him down fruitless paths but still he said he knew there was more to be discovered. At one point he picked up a handful of sand and let it fall through his fingers. He said to me, 'That is what God is like. Just as you think you have grasped God you discover that God has slipped through your fingers and you have to search yet again.' While I might not have agreed with him about main line religion - although he did have some valuable points - that image and all it meant has remained with me to this day.

I remember him sighing deeply and then saying almost to himself, 'But where can I run, you have ensnared me O God.' We walked back to the house virtually in silence but I'll be ever grateful for what he taught me that day.

So, the book of Genesis opens with a highly structured, almost hymn-like account of creation by the Priestly author. Remember that it is there to lead you into mystery, into a place where all you can do is give thanks.

Scholars eventually decided there were at least three different authors who contributed to the formation of the book of Genesis. These are identified as the Yahwist, Elohist and Priestly authors. The Yahwist is the earliest of the sources, originating in the tenth century BC, the age of David and Solomon. For the Yahwist, God is actively involved in the history of humanity and, in particular, in Israel's history. The Elohist is generally dated to the ninth century BC and is believed to have originated in the northern kingdom. The Elohist source has been so intertwined with the Yahwist that it is difficult to separate the two. The Elohist resorts to dreams and angels as means of divine communication rather than allowing direct contact with God.

The Priestly author is dated during the period of the Babylonian Exile about 550 BC but the sources used by this author come from a much earlier period. The Priestly style tends to be repetitive, and his stories are rigidly structured, giving a very solemn tone to his work. Genesis opens with the Priestly account of creation.

It runs from 1:1-2:3 where God turns chaos into order. There are similarities between this account and the Babylonian creation account, the Enuma Elish, but the author has reinterpreted and rewritten the ancient myth to reflect Israel's distinctive theology and relationship with God. In contrast to the Enuma Elish, creation does not result from conflict. There is no war between the gods, there is nothing that opposes God. Instead we are told that God creates the world in a carefully ordered sequence and it is very beautifully put together.

The opening verse tells us that before God's creative act the world was a formless void, existing as a watery chaos. This description of the world is in keeping with the beliefs and mythology of the ancient Near Eastern peoples.

The first act of creation is light, even though the sun and the moon are not created until the fourth day. The author is not concerned with scientific fact but with an ordered universe, and light is necessary in order to see. God names the light 'day,' and the darkness 'night' (v.5).

In ancient Israel, naming signified power over that which was named. God is the only one who can name the day and night because God and God alone is the only one who has authority and power over them. In just the same way and with the same inference, God will name the sky and the earth and the sea, The light is seen as good, as is the entire created universe. So the invitation is to give thanks for the gift of light, for that which illuminates the darkness. John will pick up this theme in the Gospel when he reveals Jesus as the light coming into the darkness and inaugurating the new creation of a different world order. In the first two chapters of John's Gospel we find a period of seven days taking place which mirrors the ancient creation story of Genesis.

God then creates the sky, which separates the waters above the heavens from the waters below. As I have already said, this understanding of the universe is one that is shared with the rest of the ancient Near Eastern world. The belief of all ancient peoples was that water surrounded the entire world and was held back only by the heavens above and the earth below. There was always a threat that it would envelop the earth, hence the later story of the flood. The sky was imagined as an upside down bowl which managed to keep the upper waters in place. This bowl had windows in it which allowed the rain, snow, or hail to fall to the earth. The waters below appeared on earth as streams, lakes, and springs.

God puts limits on the water so that earth can appear. From the earth God calls forth vegetation with seeds so that it is able to reproduce itself. Then on the sixth day we discover that the animals and humanity are created to inhabit the earth, which was created on the third day. It almost invites you to enter into a great song of praise to give thanks for the earth that we live on, and for the creatures that inhabit the earth. Pope Francis recently wrote an encyclical in praise of creation, called *Laudete Si,* where he reminds us to be good stewards of what we have been given.

The whole creation account has been leading up to the creation of humanity in 1:26-31. The world has been created in which humanity will live; time has been created as a measure by which humanity can govern its life. And finally man and woman are created in the image of God. Just imagine, you bear within you the image of the creator. It is the most extraordinary validation of humanity. We are not an accident. We are made in the image of God. Always give thanks for the creation of humanity, for the love of God which is for ever creative and at work in the world In the ancient world, the word 'image' was used to refer to a statue of a king which was sent to the distant corners of the kingdom where the king could not be present in person. This 'image' was to be the representative of the king in that area. To be created in the image of God is to be God's representative on earth.

How might we be seen to represent God? Surely it must be in the way we treat one another, care for one another and look after this world that we have been given and all of it is to be characterised with a spirit of thanksgiving because everything is good.

One of my mum's closest friends was a priest called John. He was a delightful man whose whole life was filled with thanksgiving. He loved people and treated everyone the same regardless of who they were. He was full of delight at the least thing he encountered always encouraging me to see goodness everywhere. He was generous to a fault. He once arrived at our house without his shoes and when my mum, horrified, pointed out his lack of footwear he looked down vaguely and then a little embarrassed told how he had met a man who did not have any shoes. He did now!

He was a simple man who did not have any need for material comfort or wealth. Money meant little to him. What he had he gave away. He had a powerful influence over me just in the way that he lived his life. He represented all that was good to me and when God found me again I saw in this man a profound icon of the reality of God.

This is why humanity is given command or dominion over the earth - so that we can be icons of the living God. Just as God is ruler of the heavenly realm, so humanity, as God's representative, is ruler of the earthly realm. This is a very exalted view of humanity. We are, as Psalm 8 tells us, little less than a God, clothed with dignity and honour. How incredible that we, with all our faults and failings, are little less than a God. Never put yourself down. Never believe the negativity that the world can place on your shoulders. You are a child of God made in God's image and likeness. If for nothing else, then learn to give thanks. I remember many years ago sitting listening to a woman, who I discovered was called Pat, telling of an encounter that she had in a doctor's surgery. She is a woman of great faith and never wastes an opportunity to share with others the love of God that she has experienced. When she entered the surgery she went to the reception, gave her name and then sat down next to another woman. It was not long before a conversation ensued. Pat had noticed that the other woman looked very sad and so she asked her how she was. The woman's very sad life story burst forth.

She told Pat about the violence that had dogged her life, some physical and some emotional. She said that never knew her father but felt his absence keenly. She shared about the sadness that she felt at her mother's rejection of her. When she married, her husband's aggression was almost too much to bear. Now that he was dead she felt that her children had given up on her and hardly ever contacted her. She said that all of it had left her with a poor self-image. She felt worthless and of no value at all. She told Pat how she dragged herself through each day and she had come to the doctor hoping for some medication to make her feel better.

Pat then shared something of her own story. She too had had an ignominious start in life. When her parents had died she had been placed in an orphanage in Ireland. She had not been well treated there at all. When her parents had died the rest of her family had been split up and some of them did not meet again until they were well on in years. Pat, because of all this had also experienced a poor self-image. It was when she was in her late thirties that she had an experience where she recognised that despite everything that had happened to her, she was of value and she mattered. Pat told the woman that she was the daughter of a king; the woman looked astonished, even more so when Pat said to her 'and so are you'. Never believe that you are less than a wonderful creation of God. Always believe in your own value because after all, you really are the son or daughter of King!

This account of creation that we have been sharing about is a theological reflection on the world that the author of Genesis has experienced. It is a world where God is seen as a powerful Being, able to create by merely speaking a word. God is seen as standing outside the universe that is called into being. Humanity is seen as the high point of creation. The world in which humanity lives has been organised by God, but as God's representative on earth, humanity is to rule over the world. It is an invitation to give thanks.

Right at the beginning of this book the theme is being developed that God alone is God and that everything has its source in God and is good. That is why the Priestly author includes the phrase over and over again, '...and God saw that it was good.'

It says something powerful about the love of God. It is the nature of God to love and love is always 'creative'. I have used that word several times. It is a word that implies energy, power and, if it comes from a loving benevolent God, then it always suggests possibility. It 'never says never'.

The world is the product of God's unfathomable creative love.

There is no way that God will ever give up on the world. Not even when we wander away or destroy the beauty of the earth. God always has a plan B. God is good and all we can do is give thanks to a God who is abundant in creation and in love.

Just recently I was in London for a meeting and since I was early I decided to walk down Piccadilly, nip into Fortnum and Mason and wander around. I cannot afford anything there but it is a great place to people watch and you do see some amazing people dressed to the nines to buy a box of tea bags. As I walked towards the shop there was a man asleep on the ground covered in sleeping bags and quilts. He and his dog were fast asleep.

Ahead of me was a very beautifully dressed businessman. As he drew near the man sleeping, he moved towards him. I thought, 'Wow, this man is going to give him something'. He did just that. He kicked him and he kicked the dog! The man, who had been asleep, was so shocked he began to cry. I have a bit of experience with people who live on the streets and I ran up and got down next to him and put my arms around him and he sobbed on my shoulder. Not only that, but all the time he sobbed the dog howled. When they had both calmed down I went and got a sandwich and coffee and some water for the dog. By the time I left they were relatively calm.

Reflecting on that incident I realised that for all our supposed compassion, we have become a hard, callous society with little compassion for the poor and vulnerable. We have forgotten the truth that we are made in the image and likeness of God and that whatever we do to another person we do to God.

I often think that the Gospel calls us into a life that is counter-cultural. The Kingdom of God where compassion, love, mercy, and forgiveness reign is meant to be real. We as followers of Jesus are meant to uphold the dignity and value of each human as having been created by God who is Good. We are to challenge the world's hardness by our gratitude for creation.

Chapter 2 of the Vatican II document *The Church in the Modern World* says that love for God cannot be separated from love for neighbour, picking up the Gospel teaching to 'love your neighbour as yourself'. The document also says, 'Everything should be rendered to a person which is required to lead a truly human life; food, clothing, shelter, the rights to freedom, education, work and respect.'

Whatever is hostile to life itself, homicide, genocide, abortion, euthanasia; whatever is offensive to human dignity, arbitrary imprisonment, slavery, prostitution; all these and the like are a disgrace and no one should be subject to them. Pope Francis in the USA a few years ago said that there can be no place in a civilised society for the death penalty.

When addressing the Senate he said, 'Therefore, all Christians and men of good will are called today to fight not only for the abolition of the death penalty, whether legal or illegal, and in all its forms, but also in order to improve the prison conditions, in respect of the human dignity of the persons deprived of freedom and I link this with a life sentence. In the Vatican, since a short time ago, there is no longer a life sentence in the penal code. A life sentence is a hidden death sentence.'

Our belief in the goodness of God and in the wonder of creation means that we have to stand against those things which would destroy God's creation and the pinnacle of that creation, man and woman. We do so with a profound belief that God is good and that creation is not an accident. It is a result of ineffable, indescribable love. So, all we can do is give thanks and treat it all as the gift that it is and every human person as the gift that they are.

The challenge for us is to trust in that reality and that is what is so hard for us. The stories in the book of Genesis are there to tell us that however it all began, God is the author. It is another way of saying that everything is gift, everything is grace. Everything comes from the goodness of God. God can make something out of nothing. God makes us what we are and gives us ourselves as his free gift. God gives us nature and creation and all of it is good and to be enjoyed. So give thanks with a grateful heart, trusting and believing in the goodness of God and the goodness and beauty of creation.

# THREE

# GIVE THANKS FOR JESUS THE CHRIST

A long time ago when I was just beginning to feel my way in the world I met a wonderful couple who lived in a town just north of Liverpool. George and Elizabeth were elderly then, but their love of the Lord was wonderful to see. It simply flowed out of them as they constantly gave thanks for the gift of their Lord and Saviour.

Theirs was a simple faith but none the less profound in its simplicity. After George died most people thought that Elizabeth would soon follow him but that did not happen. Instead, she busied herself with charity work and was one of the founders of an African charity that responded to the needs of street children. Elizabeth reached the ripe old age of 101 and until the day she died she always gave thanks for the gift of Jesus.

I was sitting with her one day and she told me of the rejection that she had experienced in her life and the reason Jesus was so important to her was that his message of love gave her a security when everyone else hated her. Her father was German and during the first world war she was sent back to Germany from London where she lived. She had a foreign accent as far as the Germans were concerned and she was isolated and bullied. She returned to London and experienced the same hatred and bullying from English children. The one place where she felt accepted, loved and cherished was in her local Methodist Church, the place her family attended on a Sunday morning. She would go and sit in the Church for hours on end, so much so that the Minister called to see her parents, he was so anxious about this child sitting alone day after day. It was there she said that her heart was filled with peace and that she discovered a love that would never leave her.

At the outbreak of the second world war she was interned in a prisoner of war camp because she had German relatives. The butcher's shop, that she and George had in London was ransacked and, after the war, when she was released, they moved up North and settled there. She and George had experienced what they called revival in the Methodist Church but eventually became Catholics in a Parish where their love for Jesus was alive and infectious. She was a wonderful woman with a heart full of thanksgiving for the gift of Jesus who had filled her with peace during the hardest times in her life. What Elizabeth had discovered in the depths of her despair was that she was loved, and that knowledge filled every fibre of her being even during her internment.

We all have to discover that truth if we are to grow in faith and know the power of God's love in our lives sustaining us and guiding us. Thank God that love does not depend on anything we do. It is an unmerited gift which is poured out upon us in an extraordinary overflow of grace from the heart of God. We are loved in our pain, in our shame, in our humiliation, in our brokenness and in our sin. We are loved in our moments of joy and laughter. We are loved when we are filled with faith and when we are haunted by doubt. We are loved despite ourselves. God is love and can only love.

I am writing this chapter while leading a retreat for priests in Easter week so my thoughts are obviously filled with the Easter story after all the celebrations of Holy week. It is a real time of thanksgiving as we reflect on Jesus' death and resurrection and what that means for us. I remember many years ago being given an Argos Poster and on it was written, 'I asked Jesus how much do you love me. 'This much' he said and stretched out his arms and died.' It was a powerful illustration of the truth of love which we see captured in the person of Jesus. God is love and will even go to the cross, that ignominious death, to show us how much we are loved. I think it was Dietrich Bonhoeffer who said that if you had been the only person in the world, Christ would still have gone to the cross so that you would know God's love for you. How can we not give thanks for this Jesus?

I want you to fast forward to what happened on that first Easter day. The Jewish Sabbath is over and the women arrive at the tomb to anoint Jesus' body. We are told that it is on the first day of the week just as the sun was rising. I love that phrase 'just as the sun was rising'. As the sun is rising out of the darkness and the light illuminates the world so, too, the Son rises from the dead, the light shining in the darkness, a light that the darkness cannot overpower. He is alive! The rising of the sun is a very evocative image.

As the women walk toward the tomb they are saying to one
another, 'Who will roll away the stone?' You know, I think that
question is as real today as it was that first Easter Day. We still
have the same human question as we struggle with our lives and
ourselves: 'Who will roll away the stone of our blockages and our
blindness, our pain and our bitterness. Who will roll away the
stone? Who will show us impossible love?'

Of course the answer to those questions in our Christian
tradition is the Risen Jesus, the lasting image and eternal icon
of what God is going to do everywhere, for everybody, now and
forever. At the very beginning of the book of Genesis you discover
that God is the creator of something out of nothing. The Spirit
hovered over the darkness and out of the chaos came order. That
is really what grace is, the desire of God, the heart of God to
make something out of nothing, to bring potential to fruition.

Richard Rohr says, 'The risen Jesus stands forever as God's
promise and guarantee of what God has always been about
and will forever be about - bringing order out of chaos, light
out of darkness, life out of death, turning crucifixions into
resurrections!' That is our hope even in the darkest places of
our lives. Jesus Christ is Lord over everything that brings death
and creates something out of nothing. It is the power of love
overflowing.

Elizabeth discovered that truth as she sat in the midst of the
darkness that she experienced and it filled her with gratitude.
Her gratitude spilled over into action as she tirelessly worked for

the poor and gave thanks to God for the gift of the Christ she found in them. Is your heart on fire with gratitude when you think of Christ, the perfect embodiment of God's love for you? In the words of Luke the evangelist, does your heart burn within you?

Jesus not only showed us the heart of God through his death and resurrection but also through his very life, a visible sign of the love of God. As we read story after story of immense compassion in the Gospels, can we do anything else but thank God that the same compassion and mercy is poured out on us? Is the challenge to be like Jesus not something else to give thanks for? Can we do anything else but thank God for the challenge that Jesus gives us to love, because that loving is what gives our lives vibrancy and meaning and draws people to the God of love.

Pope Francis in his Apostolic Exhortation *The Joy of the Gospel* wrote this, 'Thanks solely to this encounter – or renewed encounter – with God's love, which blossoms into an enriching friendship, we are liberated from our narrowness and self-absorption. We become fully human when we become more than human, when we let God bring us beyond ourselves in order to attain the fullest truth of our being. Here we find the source and inspiration of all our efforts at evangelisation. For if we have received the love which restores meaning to our lives, how can we fail to share that love with others?'

So Jesus' life, death and resurrection is a cause of thanksgiving, and impels us to share the love that we see in him. You know, if you really reflect on who Jesus is you discover a radical free man driven by the wildness of the spirit who allowed the love of God to flow through him. His was a heart that was full of gratitude for the gift of life and for the revelation of the presence of God in the world. His was a heart overflowing in thanksgiving and who invites us to be the same.

That is our primary challenge, then, not to let suspicion, doubt, or fear of otherness cloud our vision. We are to live as Jesus lived, full of gratitude at the wonder of life and, through that gratitude, to share with others the cause of our joy.

When I was a university chaplain many years ago I used to take groups of students to visit the Poor Clares when they still had a community in Liverpool. There is a little bit of mystique surrounding enclosed orders and the students were always fascinated by the sisters' lifestyle. It seemed to many of them a real waste of time to shut yourself off from the world and pray for the world.

I always found it interesting how the buzz of chatter on the minibus would grind to a halt when we went through the gates to the monastery which would shut behind us. We would then be taken to the parlour by a silent extern sister. There we would wait for the other sisters to arrive. I think the students wondered if we would ever get out.

On one visit, the sisters came into the parlour and began to introduce themselves. There was one ancient looking lady who beamed around at us all and introduced herself as Sister Mary Francis. Almost as one, the other sisters turned around to her and said 'No you are not. We have told you this before'. It was very funny at the time but what struck me forcibly was the joy that exuded from those sisters. It was almost tangible even from the one who did not quite know who she was. It was their relationship with Christ that filled those sisters with gratitude and his revelation of God's love that flowed from them in their simplicity.

In order to be filled with gratitude, we somehow have to be open to the sort of relationship with God that Jesus had, a relationship in which we allow God to take over our hearts, and allow ourselves to hand over control. It is an invitation to let go and surrender ourselves. That relationship is what fills us with gratitude. When we realise that we depend on God for our very existence, we can only be grateful.

That relationship then leads us into relationship with the world and with our brothers and sisters. So, discover how to be in relationship with God and then discover how to be in relationship with the brothers and sisters and then with the world. Try to live in the gift of the moment that you have been given. Recognise that the world is a gift given for you to live in and you will live in that deep gratitude that cannot be overcome. That is the example of Jesus and that is why we can be thankful for him.

To live life in gratitude means to live a life filled with purpose. Jesus, after his Baptism, knew his vocation in life - to reveal to others the God he had encountered in the desert, an encounter that filled him with gratitude. Our call is to live, like he did, a life that has meaning and purpose, a life that is full of gratitude. We are not meant to live superficial lives but lives of deep gratitude to God for love and to give our lives in service for what we have received.

It's that gratitude that I often see in the Scriptures. People encounter the Lord, experience healing and freedom and are filled with joy and thanksgiving. Think of the story of the Samaritan woman, or the story of Zacchaeus or the story of the one leper who came back to say thank you. That gratitude joy and thanksgiving only happens when encounters with the Lord take place.

One of my favourite stories in the Scriptures is the story of the healing of Jairus' daughter which has the story of the woman with the haemorrhage in the middle of it. It is a great story of encounter. Recently I was in the Holy Land and while there visited Magdala. It was the first time I had ever been there. The excavations have been taking place for some time but only recently has the site been opened. It was quite a small place with a magnificent Church overlooking the sea of Galilee. While we were there we were taken down in to the crypt under the boat shaped Church with the magnificent views.

On the wall there was a beautiful painting of the woman who had been bleeding for many years reaching out to touch the hem of Jesus' cloak. This was her moment of encounter. You might remember the story. Jesus is approached by a man named Jairus, who asks him to come and cure his daughter who is at home, sick. As Jesus made his way to Jairus' house, with a curious crowd all around him a woman who, we are told, had been bleeding for eighteen years and had spent all her money on doctors without getting any better, approached him very quietly. I often try to imagine how she must have felt and the courage it took for her, an unclean woman, to go into a crowd of people. What faith and trust! It seems she was saying to herself: 'If I just touch the hem of his cloak, I will be healed!' The painting in Magdala only shows the woman's hand reaching through the crowd at foot level as she tries to touch the hem of his cloak. We know the story; she does just that and instantly she is healed, the bleeding stops and she is well again. That touching of Jesus did for her what doctors could not do: it stopped bleeding. I am reminded of the wonderful Godfrey Birtill song *Just one touch from the King changes everything*. I guess she must have been filled with joy after that her encounter with the Lord.

Then, as Jesus is approaching Jairus' house, he is told that the man's daughter is already dead. He enters into the house anyway, goes to the young girl's bed, takes her by the hand, and brings her back to life. Again what rejoicing and deep gratitude there must have been.

These two women have something in common. For different reasons, both are unable to give life; the young girl, because she dies, just as she is about to become a woman and has the possibility of getting pregnant, and the other woman, because

her body was damaged and haemorrhaging, making it impossible
for her to have a child.

What Jesus does is give back to both women the possibility of
giving life, in one case by stopping the flow of blood and in the
other by starting it. What joy must have filled their hearts.

We all need something similar to happen to us. Often there are
deep parts of us which have died and are too cold and lifeless to
ever bring life to anything. Like the woman whose internal
bleeding was making her sick and weak, we too are wounded in
ways that have us forever haemorrhaging and we become cynical
and sad, dominated by our pain, unable to break free and bring
life to others. Parts of us have died and parts of us have been
wounded and we are forever haemorrhaging in body, heart, and
soul. It is very hard for us to give life.

In the end, the power to give life can only be restored to us
through grace, through letting a power beyond give us something
that we cannot give to ourselves. Then will those parts of us that
are dead or diseased begin again to give life and we will give
thanks. We have to encounter Jesus, the icon of God, in order to
bring life and what gratitude that brings.

It always strikes me that whenever there is an encounter with
Jesus, change takes place. There is new awareness, new
awakening, new sight. Both of those women changed. When that
happens to you, you can only be grateful. If we are to live life to
the full, with a real sense of gratitude then maybe the invitation

is to allow God to fill us and free us to know the truth of who we are and what the world is.

I am sure that anyone reading this will know the story of a Christmas Carol by Charles Dickens. When the curtains of his life are pulled back, Scrooge finally grasps how selfish, power hungry, and evil he has become. When The Ghost of Christmas Yet to Come shows Scrooge that he will die with no one mourning his death, it shocks him into negotiating for one last chance. As Scrooge begins to live out of his new heart, he produces new fruit, generous concern for the poor, and a heart full of gratitude and joy. His cynicism, narrowness and hardness are vanquished. After our encounter with the Lord, we too can be filled with gratitude and joy.

So what are the characteristics of someone who has this sense of gratitude and lives out the kingdom life? I certainly recognised something in Elizabeth but maybe we have to look at the personality of Jesus that comes to us through the Scriptures. I think you probably have to read behind the words and stories to discover this.

Primarily Jesus is joyful with a deep-rooted joy that can never be taken from him. I remember a sister once giving me a picture called the laughing Jesus. His head is thrown back and the joy seems to flow from him as he laughs out loud and long. He seemed to be always at the centre of dinner parties and weddings. Life is not an endurance test for Jesus but something to be embraced and lived to the full. In his experience in the desert after his Baptism, he knew at a foundational level that he was secure in the love that flowed from the heart of God for him. That meant he could sit with tax collectors and sinners and wonder at all the fuss it caused. It meant he could touch lepers and the unclean. His sense of security shows us that it is alright to challenge others when challenge is needed. He was full of compassion and mercy. He was alive to the moment which meant his attention was always on the people he was with. His temple, his place of worship, was wherever he was at the time, in a garden, at a party, with the sick or the sinner because wherever he was he encountered the reality of God.

Jesus was someone who was open to otherness, and was not forever judging and blaming others for the state of the world, the occupation of the Romans or indeed anything else. He seemed to be able to live at peace with even those who do not see life in quite the way that he did. He was more alive and human than any other human being that has ever lived. For that example of what it means to be human and alive surely we can give thanks to God?

I have seen that fulness of life in so many people that I have met down the years, people who have walked in faith and encountered the Lord in their lives. They are always wonderfully grateful and aware of God with them. However, one stands out for me more than anyone else. Although I hesitate to say that because I am always being surprised by people who despite the circumstances they live in try, day in and day out, to follow the example of Jesus and live their lives in gratitude.

The person I am thinking about is Hannah. Hannah was a friend of my mother and also the head teacher of the local infants' school where both my brother Paul and I attended. She is now one hundred and three years old and lives in a retirement home. Throughout my life Hannah has always been a wonderful example of what it means to be a Christian. She is extraordinarily generous. Many poor children in her school were clothed and fed by Hannah down the years. Even in the 1960's, in Hannah's school there was a breakfast club before they became popular. Her generosity extended to me. I remember when I was seven. It was New Year's Eve and my mum and dad were having a party. I was put to bed just before the guests began to arrive. I lay, listening to people arriving and the laughter and conversation going on in the hall outside my bedroom. I have to say I felt pretty miserable. I wanted to go to the party and eat the food and dance. As I lay there feeling sorry for myself, the door opened and my mum came in with Hannah who wanted to see me and as she gave me a kiss goodnight she pressed a piece of paper into my hand. It was a ten shilling note. I would be surprised if I had ever seen one before. As I looked at it, with wide open eyes, it was taken out of my hands by mum who promised to look after it for me. I cannot remember if I ever saw it again but for those few seconds, Hannah's generosity made me feel like the richest kid in town.

Hannah served the parish community through the school for most of her working life, always full of joy with a listening ear and an obviously glad heart. She laughed and smiled her way through the school year. In her office was a huge jar of sweets and every child, even when they had been naughty, was a recipient. She had a cupboard full of clothes and shoes so that the poorer children did not feel disadvantaged by what they had to wear. After she retired she worked tirelessly for the poor through the legion of Mary and at the same time, looked after her brother James and sister Mary until the day they died. She was commissioned as a Eucharistic Minister when she was ninety so that she could take them holy communion. The tears of joy that tripped down her face that day were a sight to behold. Hannah moved into the home she now lives in when she was one hundred and one. She fell and broke her hip and gratitude is still the hallmark of her life. She is always smiling, always grateful and still a joy to be with.

Gratitude has filled her life and gratitude for her Lord and Saviour has constantly spilled over into her love and concern for others. Her life has been full and happy and she has touched the hearts and minds of more people than I care to imagine. That has made Hannah a very full rounded human being and I thank God for her example.

So give thanks for the gift of Jesus the Christ. Give thanks for your encounters with him that have turned you round and filled you with joy. Be grateful for the example he gives of the fullness of humanity, and as you open your heart to him let your gratitude spill over and touch the lives of others.

I would like to finish this chapter with some words of Richard Rohr: 'We have committed ourselves to gratitude. We have come to realise that those who make space for gratitude, those who prefer nothing to gratitude, will most assuredly have it. To be a Christian is to be 'burdened' with gratitude. We must not be afraid to share it with immigrants, slum dwellers, saddened prisoners, angry prophets. Now and then we must even announce it to ourselves. In this prison of now, in this cynical and sophisticated age, Christians must believe in gratitude or they do not believe in the God of Jesus.'

# FOUR

# GIVE THANKS FOR
# THE PRESENCE OF THE SPIRIT

One of my abiding memories is of a visit that took place to Mull and Iona some years go. I stayed on Mull with a friend and there were many memorable occasions. In the cottage where we stayed, there was a window that ran the length of it and every morning we would get up fairly early and would not speak to each other but just look out of the window and watch the colours changing on the water and the birds beginning to sing. It was an incredible experience.

One of the mornings as I sat there, I realised that the scenery I was looking at was unchanging but my attitude towards that beauty was changing. As the light touched the water and changed its colour, it was my attitude towards that water that changed and not the water itself. I began to get a sense of the Spirit changing me within as I looked and began to see so many things in my life in a different way.

Another day in the week was spent on Iona. We had a look around and then went our separate ways. I found myself on a beach. It was completely isolated and so I settled down and looked out at the sea and just became aware of the gift of that moment and the Spirit, hovering, challenging me to live in the moment and not just in my head. I looked at my watch and two hours had gone in a flash. It was, again, an experience of the Spirit of God which went beyond words.

I often think that the Spirit of God is the least reflected on aspect of God because it is so difficult to tie the Spirit down and most of us want to do that. We want to make the Spirit comfortable when the Spirit is anything but comfortable. Pope Francis recently wrote this; 'To put it simply: the Holy Spirit bothers us because he moves us, he makes us walk, he pushes the church to go forward, and we are like Peter at the transfiguration: 'Ah, how wonderful it is to be here like this, all together!' ... but don't bother us. We want the Holy Spirit to doze off. We want to domesticate the Holy Spirit and that is no good, because he is God. He is that wind which comes and goes and you do not know where. He is the power of God; he is the one who gives us consolation and strength to move forward. But, to move forward, and this bothers us. It is so much nicer to be comfortable.'

I returned from that trip to Mull and Iona a different person than I had been before. During my time there, I had become aware of the presence of something more than I am. This presence led me deeply into an awareness of who I am and who God is, which has to be the work of the creating, moving Spirit of God.

I have been fascinated over the last few years by two questions that I think are right at the heart of the Scriptures, 'Who am I?' and 'Who are you?' It is hard to look at who we are with our small-minded pettiness. It is even harder to look at how God sees us which is truly who we are, beloved, and realise how much the Spirit has to do to move us to that place. It is difficult to let God reveal Godself to us because that catapults us into an untidy, messy place where we are not in control.

I think that is why most of us see the Scriptures as being about information rather than transformation, when in fact the opposite is true. The Scriptures are inviting us to reflect on those two questions so that the work of Spirit, which is always to transform, can begin. As long as you treat the Scriptures as sources of information then you will always be at a distance from what God wants to do. What is it that God wants to do? I think it is to tell us who we really are and who God really is.

As Christians what we have to offer the world is the discovery of what it means to be really human and alive and that is intimately connected with this God who is life giving. It is to know the truth of who we are in God's sight and who God is for us. So, it is the way we walk the journey and discover meaning through the journey we walk. It is the way that we are faithful to discovery and to journey that leads us deeply into those questions. The answers we discover become truth to live by because it takes us deeply into the meaning of our humanity and our divinity. In that discovery, we no longer have to protect or blame but can simply be happy to be.

In that walking of the journey we will most surely find the God of meaning who is present, the God of overwhelming mercy, compassion and love. The God who weeps and the God who laughs. The God who is with us in the midst of our humanity. When we find the God who is present, then we'll have truth to share with the world. All of it is the work of the Spirit and, while it is not easy, it has to be something which it is right to give thanks for.

I would like to spend part of this Chapter reflecting on Jesus' conversation with Nicodemus and then move to several other places in John's Gospel where we are invited to reflect on the Spirit. The encounter between Jesus and Nicodemus can be found in John Chapter three. Nicodemus came by night to see Jesus. The evangelist mentions 'at night' probably to signify that Nicodemus was in the dark, that is, he was not open to the presence of the Spirit and also was consumed by the fear that other religious leaders might find out about this visit. I think it is probable that some of the Jewish leaders were already getting upset about Jesus' activities and his teaching that was changing people's lives.

Jesus' conversation with Nicodemus is about the reality of the Spirit. It is interesting that John places it immediately after the story of the wedding at Cana. Somehow all the symbolism of new wine and new life seems to point towards the Spirit. John wants us to know that life is given from above. We cannot create ourselves. We come to know who we are because of the relationships that we enter into. We come to know who we are through others. If you want to know fully who you are then let God tell you. Let God create you from above. If you want to know who God is let the same process take place.

Nicodemus misunderstands. John often uses misunderstanding scenes in the Gospel to move us beyond the initial question to the deeper truth he wants us to know. So, when Nicodemus asks his question, 'How can a grown man be born again,' Jesus begins to teach us about the Spirit. The wind is a symbol of the Spirit and John wants us to know that creating Spirit in our lives cannot be controlled and monitored. Like the wind, you only see its effects as people are brought to life. You have to let it move as you will. Rob Bell, the evangelical preacher, once said, 'the moment God is figured out with nice neat lines and definitions, we are no longer dealing with God. Love is giving up control. It is surrendering the desire to control the other person. The two - love and controlling power over the other person - are mutually exclusive. If we are serious about loving someone, we have to surrender all the desires within us to manipulate the relationship.'

Most of the time we are afraid to let the Spirit move at will because of where that might lead us. It is scary to hand over control, and yet Jesus tells us it is the only way to fully know who we are and who God is.

One of the interesting challenges to Nicodemus and I think to all of us, is the way in which John sees the Spirit as blowing wherever the Spirit will. Nicodemus is very sure of himself. He knows that he is a teacher of the law, he knows his own identity and he knows who God is. This is because he is theologically trained and understands the law. It gives him a security and, as a Pharisee, power over others. Having said that, there is

something wonderful about Nicodemus because he is searching
for more, and while he is a bit frightened about what he might
find, he wants more. There is a battle going on within him and
 he wants to make a judgment about Jesus and his teaching.

As the conversation begins, it becomes clear that Nicodemus is
way out of his depth. Despite his training and his certainty, he
is being challenged to let go of it all and begin to see in a
different way. He is going to see who he is with a whole new
depth of understanding and he is going to have to see who God
is in another way too. It must have scared the life out of
Nicodemus. Everything he had been taught and by which he had
made sense of his life was being challenged. To be born from
above as Jesus seems to understand it means becoming like a
child again. It is about discovering in the depth of our being that
we are children of God, listening to the Spirit of God, and letting
ourselves be guided by the Spirit.

Henri Nouwen once wrote, 'Any dance of celebration must weave
both the sorrows and the blessings into a joyful step.... to heal is
to let the Holy Spirit call me to dance, to believe again, even
amid my pain, that God will orchestrate and guide my life.'

I remember meeting a woman called Marie who was a retired
doctor. She had sold her house and moved into a caravan
somewhere up in Scotland. She bought a van and spent most of
her time running a mobile clinic on the streets and in homeless
shelters. She did it because she had a dream in which she had
an encounter with a homeless man. He said to her in her dream,

'I am Christ, how are you touching me.' The dream left her profoundly disturbed and aware that she was being prompted by the Spirit. It was against all advice that she did what she did, and yet countless people have been helped because she allowed the Spirit to lead her and guide her.

I think the Spirit scares the life out of most of us because to be certain is to be secure, to be open is to be vulnerable, and none of us really want that in our lives. Despite that fear, I often think that there is a desire to be born again in many of us. Often we want to start afresh, to leave behind past hurts, habits and old ways that imprison us. Often we want to turn away from the values of our society which can prevent us from growing towards greater freedom. The message of Jesus is about transformation, emerging from all of that into something new which promises life so vibrant and full that we can hardly breathe. That is why we are to give thanks for the Spirit because the Spirit will rebirth us into new life.

Nicodemus then asks the question 'How is this new birth going to come about?' Nicodemus, this Jewish teacher who is sure of himself and of his theology, has had his very foundations rocked and he does not really know what to do. However he senses something here in this encounter and he asks, 'How can this happen?'

Jesus is shocked at his question: 'Are you a teacher in Israel and yet you do not understand these things?' Jesus seems to be inviting Nicodemus to look at the law and the prophets and to see the truth that lies there. All the great Hebrew prophets had announced the gift of the Spirit of God that would renew people and change their hearts. This gift of the Spirit and of life announced by the prophets is often symbolised by water because water cleanses, purifies and gives life. The prophet Ezekiel saw the waters flowing from the New Temple which brought healing and gave life. The prophet Joel had announced that the Spirit of God would be poured out - not just on the religious leaders, prophets and theologians, but on all the people. How could Nicodemus forget all the promises of God revealed through the prophets? As Jean Vanier says in his book *Drawn into the Mystery of Jesus through the Gospel of John*, 'What made him cling to human religious ways and theological certitudes devoid of the wind, of the breath of the Spirit, which made him blind to the new ways of God?' We have to ask the questions: What makes us blind to the ways of God and to the new thing that God wants to do? What makes us cling desperately to our own ideas and plans, to religion that does not bring life?

In response to Nicodemus, Jesus reveals that he is the one who has come to fulfil the word of God announced by the prophets. He is the one who will give us this new life in the Spirit. To find it, we are called to let go of traditions which are self-serving, of images of God which lead us from the truth, of our desperate need to be right and to know, in order to live by the Spirit of Jesus.

I would like to leave Nicodemus there and move to another place in John's Gospel. After chapter thirteen in the Gospel which is a turning point, John spends a lot of time going over various themes that he's introduced in the Gospel and so he reflects on the Spirit several times.

In chapter fourteen, Jesus reminds the disciples and us that he will be with us; the advocate will come to be our defender. In Greek, the word for advocate is Paraclete. A Paraclete was one who stood by those who were unable to speak for themselves, and fought their case in a court of law.

We are being invited to trust in that ever present Paraclete. The question always is about our willingness to surrender and let go and allow this Paraclete to be with us in a real and experiential way. Do we trust the presence of God within us? Do we trust that God is more on our side that we are on own side? Do we believe that God is good?

Richard Rohr says, 'But why would we entrust ourselves to someone that we do not know, or that we do not know is inherently good, or we are not sure is even on our side? It is the Holy Spirit, the inner Paraclete who prompts us to trust beyond ourselves, who teaches us that God is good, and that God is more for us than we are for ourselves.'

The Spirit of the absent Jesus will be the Paraclete, to be with us and to help us as we face the world. The Paraclete will teach us that God is good and more on our side than we care to imagine. We are not alone or alien because the Spirit is with us. That is how intimate the relationship is between us and this God.

John then tells that the response to the knowledge of this indwelling love is peace that the world cannot give or take away. Is that not something to give thanks for?

We move now into Chapter sixteen to find more about the Spirit. Chapter sixteen is almost like a re-run of chapter fourteen as we begin to look again at the reality of the Spirit and the promise of the Spirit's coming. We are told that the Spirit will reveal truth and bring an end to injustice and evil. The Spirit will show us what sin is. We do not know what sin is and often think that our guilt is in some way a criterion for sin. For John there is only one sin and that is not to know your father. Everything we call sin is simply a symptom of not knowing. The Spirit will teach us what judgement is about, not our petty understanding, not vengeance or revenge but about love and life and respecting choice. The Spirit will teach us as time goes on.... 'there are many things that I still have to say to you but they would be too much for you now.' The disciples then begin to understand, and Jesus says that understanding will help them through their times of trial and misunderstanding in the world. He tells them that there will be trouble but to be brave because your experience of the Lord will take you through. The advocate will take you through to victory so do not be afraid. Give thanks for the presence of the Spirit within you.

So let us look now at Chapter twenty. The Gospel is drawn together here in the resurrection story. It becomes for us the eternal sign of hope. We know that love is victorious. Chapter twenty begins with the story of the empty tomb. Peter and John come running to the tomb and we find that love, John, arrived at the tomb first. It is love that will understand the resurrection. John waits and lets Peter enter first. They find the empty tomb, which is not a proof of resurrection. The empty grave clothes show us that Jesus no longer had any need for earthly trappings. For John only the personal experience of the risen Jesus is proof of resurrection. The insight of love is what will recognise the things of God. There are different ways of seeing. The Spirit will enable us to see, so give thanks.

We then find John the evangelist telling us of the first appearance of the risen Jesus to Mary of Magdalene and he shows how Jesus is only available to a new kind of sight in that encounter. What was it she was looking for in the garden that she could not quite see and recognise the risen Jesus? She was looking for a dead body, and the truth is that we only really see what we are looking for. If you are looking for the risen Lord, you will see him. So Mary could not see the truth that Jesus was present, maybe in the flesh and blood of a gardener, because she was not looking for him there.

It is John's way of saying to us that this risen Lord is present in a new and very real way but we have to open our eyes and see him. We have to allow this risen Jesus to break through the petty limitations that we put on him and reveal his presence. Mary, let go of what you thought you had, to discover what you really have. It is a powerful illustration of what life is about, the process of letting go to discover the real. We all have to do it, let go of our image of God, of our presumptions about where we will find

God and look again with fresh eyes. That is where the Spirit is at work, and when it happens we can do nothing but be grateful. Mary of Magdala heard her name called in the depth of her heart and she then began to see with the eyes of faith and she ran and proclaimed the truth that he's alive and with us. The Disciples do not believe her. They are frightened, gathered together trying to find comfort and help from one another. In verse 20 Jesus came and stood among them. Once again John is trying to show us a new kind of presence. It is a presence that can come through closed doors and is among us. It is a presence outside space or time and his greeting to them is Shalom, a word that for the Jews promises fulfilment. In his presence we can find complete fulfilment. Then he shows them his hands and his side. The risen Jesus is still the wounded Jesus. It is a symbol of humanity. We enter into eternity in our wounded state. He brings his wounded humanity before the Father and trusts in the Father's love. That is what we do and his gaze of love will bring us to wholeness and peace. Then we will finally know that we do not have to be perfect to be loved. We just have to trust and believe in his love, and in this love our sin is forgotten. It is the work of the Spirit and a wonderful revelation to give thanks for.

That is why John couples the breathing of the Spirit with the forgiveness of sins. We are told that Jesus breathed on the disciples and said, 'Receive the Holy Spirit for those whose sins you forgive they are forgiven, for those who sins you retain they are retained.' This is John's Pentecost scene. Everything happens for John on the first day of the week. It is the kairos moment, the significant moment. The Spirit is given and it is all about forgiveness. When are we going to believe that we are forgiven? When we allow the Spirit to be breathed on us. When we know and believe that we are loved, then our sinfulness no longer matters. The forgiveness of sin is about a relationship of love. Our hope in the resurrection is that God will be God; that God will be the kind of lover that we understand. He was for Jesus and so will be for us. The power of forgiveness is given to all Disciples. We have limited the experience that John wants us all to have to priesthood, but our Sacrament is a celebration of what we live. Without forgiveness there is no real life amongst the Community.

We then read the story of Thomas, a story that calls us to a deeper level of believing. We do not have to see with physical eyes to enter into relationship with Jesus and to believe that life comes from death. It is a different kind of sight. The Disciples, despite their experience, stay locked up in fear and anxiety. Jesus comes into their midst and again says 'Shalom', and then we find after all that has gone on for twenty chapters the moment of affirmation from the mouth of a disciple. Thomas says, 'My Lord and My God.' He is the man who can now see. Incredible faith! It is the Spirit that leads us to that place of faith where we say my Lord and my God. Again, when we realise that truth, we can only give thanks.

It struck me when I was thinking about this story of Thomas that God has grown accustomed to our fearful ways of waiting behind closed doors; doors that are made up of our fear, anxiety and self-doubt. God knows how easily we settle for those things rather than Gospel freedom. God knows how most of us seem to want a very small God instead of a big mystery. Check out Nicodemus again. Yet God seems determined to break through: 'And Jesus came and stood in their midst and said, 'Peace!'" The Spirit that is breathed on us eventually overcomes the obstacles that we present and surrounds us with enough peace so that we can, like Thomas, say, 'My Lord and my God'.

So the Spirit is very much present in the Gospel of John, underpinning everything that happens and challenging us. Are you willing to be born from above? Are you willing to be open to the Spirit? Are you prepared to let go of what you think you know to discover a much bigger picture? That is the challenge of the Spirit in John's Gospel. What you do with that challenge is up to you. If you open yourself up and allow yourself to be born from above, your life will become one of gratitude and praise for the gift of the Spirit.

# FIVE

# GIVE THANKS FOR THE WONDER OF YOUR BEING

S onia is a social worker I met at a conference in Glasgow some years ago. She is married with four children and her husband is a teacher, a deputy head in a Catholic Primary school. We had a couple of conversations during the week-long conference and then everybody went their separate ways.

About three weeks later I got an email from Sonia asking could she come and see me. I was intrigued by this and wondered why she wanted to come but agreed to meet with her. She got the train from Scotland and eventually arrived. She had friends in Liverpool who she was going to stay with that evening.

As soon as she walked through the door I could sense there was something badly wrong. She was very tense and anxious. She was nervously twisting her hands together and her voice sounded taut and strange. We sat down and she started to cry so I just sat and waited for the storm to subside. I have learnt over the years that touching someone in that sort of state is not always welcome and often words provide no comfort. When she stopped crying I smiled at her and asked her what the tears were about. She immediately started to cry again and as she cried, she told me that she was a bad mother and that her children hated her because she had let them down. She could not tell me how; she really did not have a reason. She said that she was a poor wife,

a terrible Christian and her career was going down the pan.
Then she looked at me and told me that she hated herself and
she had thought of taking her own life because everybody would
be better off without her.

I am very glad that these days Sonia is in a much better place
but at that time she was unable to recognise that she was a
wonderful, unique creation of God. She was unable to see that
she was gift; to herself, to her family, to the people she worked
with and to her clients.

It is amazing how often I have come across similar scenarios.
I have met many people who seem to have it altogether and
yet deep within have a lurking insecurity and are unable to
recognise, and therefore rejoice, in the wonder of their being.

When reflecting on the beauty of creation, I named humanity as
the pinnacle of God's creation and in the last chapter reflected
on Jesus as the icon of God and the icon for the fullness of
humanity. As he is, so should we be. O for the grace to see
ourselves as God sees us. O for the gift of being able to rejoice in
the wonder of our being and to give thanks.

A few years ago, I was working with a group of doctors and
nurses from the Merseyside Palliative Care Trust. We were
looking at how we could assess spiritual need in patients who
had a terminal illness. As we began, I asked them, 'What is
spirituality?'

They came back with some wonderful statements like: the very stuff of life; the glue that holds everything together; the essence of who we are; indefinable and indescribable but there; something which is in us and yet beyond us. I thought that was a good response from a group of people several of whom would say they were atheists.

In his book *Seeking Spirituality* Ronald Rolheiser says: 'spirituality is not about serenely picking or rationally choosing certain spiritual activities like going to church, praying or meditating, reading spiritual books or setting off on some explicit spiritual quest. It is far more basic than that. Long before we do anything explicitly religious at all, we have to do something about the fire that burns within us.'

It is only when we get in touch with that fire within that we begin to recognise what incredible beings we are. That is what spirituality is all about; how we make sense of that basic fire for life that is within every human person. Not to be spiritual means we have lost that basic desire to live life to the full. It means we are not energised by the world we live in. I sometimes think that many in the Church are religious people but not spiritual people because often we use religion to subjugate that basic desire for life. I once had a lecturer at College who used to say that most people look at the Church and hear, 'In the beginning was the word and the word was 'No'.' Yet, right at the heart of faith is the truth that God created every human person out of love and our human nature is an extraordinary gift. God said a great big 'Yes' to creation and to humanity. As Church we should be trying to help people discover what the fullness of humanity looks like.

In the last thirty years the New Age culture has developed because people are looking for something to help them to make sense of that inner fire. What did Jesus say? 'The harvest is rich, but the labourers are few.' We are the labourers in a harvest that is there for the picking; but the truth is we are not going to attract people unless our spirituality is authentic, and unless it is deeply and profoundly human. We are not going to attract people until we help them really understand how fantastic they are. It is the nature of who we are that attracts people and influences people. Our awareness of our own spirituality and our development in the understanding of how marvellous we are is of vital importance in the whole area of authentic evangelisation.

If you want to begin to understand the value and dignity of humanity, take a moment to reflect on the incarnation. God became flesh. God did not remain Spirit. God became flesh and in doing so made our humanity holy. Whatever you were taught in the past about enduring this world for the sake of the next, is not Christian truth. It is a parody of that truth. The material matters: it is important in God's eyes so we have to explore what it means to be human and learn how to give thanks. I love the phrase that Ronald Rolheiser uses when he describes the incarnation as a multifaceted diamond turning in the sun. What a beautiful reflection which enables us to recognise that one of those facets is the value of the flesh, the material, the sensual, the physical. We matter; I matter, you matter. It is the most freeing reality you can ever discover.

Sadly we as Christians have often pushed ourselves into a corner where we are seen as being anti-materialistic, anti-sensual, anti-body, anti-sexual, anti-physical pleasure, and anti-erotic, which often means we avoid being real and escape into a false spirituality where we become narrow, frowning people who have little joy and who can live false protected lives. We seem reluctant to love the physical. 'Do not laugh in Church, do not talk.' We devalue what it means to be human beings when the centre of our faith is all about 'the word made flesh'.

I think the invitation we are given is to be real, loving and honouring our lives and our humanity. Our task as church is to help nourish and protect the goodness of humanity to the world that's often hostile to us. We have to be real.

I have discovered over the years that I have been working in retreat centres, and particularly over the last years with groups of all sorts, that people are desperately searching for meaning and for life deep within. It is a cry that some of us have not identified yet because we are so well protected and covered up.

We have to get to grips with the inner life so that we can offer the world the real wisdom that can be found in Jesus and in his way. Any other solution is just a panacea and does not offer real life. The wisdom of Christian spirituality is that it does offer a life that is rich, vibrant and fulfilling. It invites us to get in touch with the spiritual centre and meet the God who has chosen to live deeply within us.

For many people spirituality has nothing to do with the human condition. It is divorced from the human. Spirituality is something we do rather than something we are. I find that very sad because the truth is that we are body, mind and spirit, whole beings.

It is why I find it so difficult when we pray at Mass that our souls be healed. I find myself asking the question 'What about the rest of me?' It is a false dichotomy to split ourselves up. We are both spiritual and physical. Give thanks for who and what we are. Give thanks for our humanity.

Our human nature is holy, in many ways damaged and broken, but holy none the less. Incarnation tells us that we must take our humanity seriously and any form of spirituality that makes us reject the reality of who we are is never going to satisfy our desire for God. We, in our humanity, reflect the nature of God. We have to take seriously who and what we are. We have to be real.

What might that mean? I think it might mean looking at everything that happens in our lives and asking questions like 'Why did I do that?' 'What was that reaction about?' It is an invitation to be honest and stop playing the games that so many of us play, pretending all the time, blaming others for what goes wrong in our lives, having to be right all the time.

The challenge is to become aware of what lies within and face whatever blocks the inner life. It is a painful process, but then nearly all growth is painful because it involves stripping away and breaking through and letting go. If we are to fully discover what it means to be human then it is a process we have to go through. We can choose not to embark on it, but to do that is to live at a superficial level only enjoying a percentage of what God has created us for. We were not created to endure life but to live it to the full. The church and prayer is to enable us to go on this journey of discovery and so find life.

Timothy Radcliffe the Dominican priest has said very powerfully, in a way that issues a challenge; 'Humans do not want love relationships; we want religion and all its trappings because that is much more comfortable. A love relationship continues to challenge and make demands. It also offers a joy that we cannot tolerate: too near, too lavish, too spacious. what might we do with such freedom?'

So do we want religion with all its trappings or do we want an intimate relationship with Christ which will lead us to love our humanity and find the presence of God in it? You can always tell when someone is into the trappings of Religion. They are usually more pious and churchy. They are not at ease with who they are. They are entangled with the need to do things properly and be right.

They can be, in the worst extremes, bigoted, judgemental and condemnatory. It is so easy for us to travel down this path and it stops us seeing the presence of God everywhere. When we stay locked into the narrow confines of our own experience judging what is right or wrong who is in and who is out we are unable to become people who are open to journey and to the discovery of the wonder in life.

I have discovered that in some extraordinary people down the years but never more so than when I met Jean Vanier, an incredibly human person full of awe at the uniqueness of every human being even the most disadvantaged. So holiness and spirituality is all tied up with a deeply profound experience of what it means to be human. When we realise that, we are filled with gratitude at the wonder of our being.

I love the film Shawshank Redemption, the story of real life in the midst of brutality. If you have never seen the film I would recommend it to you. It lets us know that in every human person, there is under the surface, beauty and wonder and we will respond to those breath-taking qualities of humanity and give thanks for them.

I think this reflection on the wonder of our being leads us to a place of vulnerability where we are not in control, where we do not have all the answers. It is a place where life is about journeying and discovering, trusting, risking, letting go and living. It takes us to a place of looking in every human life for goodness and that can be hard to do when we have been hurt, let down or traumatised in some way by another child of God.

Over the years that I have been in ministry, I have sensed a call to holiness, not a false piety, but a real earthy human reality that knows the truth that God is in all things. It recognises that God is even in the mess and there has probably been a lot of mess in all our lives. When we see the presence of God in a messy, broken life we can give thanks for the immense privilege of being human and being graced by God.

Many years ago I was given a verse called *We Told our Stories*. It is written by Edwina Gately. There is one line in it which always speaks powerfully to me. It goes like this: 'In each muddy twisted path, God's gentle life broke through and we heard music in the dark and smelt flowers in the void.' It is beautiful, that whatever may have happened in our lives, God is present. Trust it, believe it, nothing is wasted, even the sin and the darkness. God is present, weeping with us and rejoicing with us and, as Saint Paul said, turning all things to good.

How do we get to that place within where we appreciate ourselves and spend our lives giving thanks for the fullness of life and the gift of humanity? I think there is a lot of letting go that has to take place if we are to be able to give thanks for the gift of our humanity. I often think there is a need to let go of some of our images of God. I have written about this before but I am certain it is true. Many of us were brought up with a very narrow understanding of a God who only deals in black and white and right and wrong. That leads to a small, petty God who frowns on humanity and who fails to delight in what has been created. We have been fed a God who judges in the way we judge and who therefore scares the life out of us. This leads to a place where life is to be endured in order to get to heaven and our humanity is something we have to put up with rather than rejoice in.

The God of Jesus is more. The God of Jesus is benevolence, abundance, life-giving, charged with awesome, incredible, ferocious love which heals, transforms and restores. There is no condemnation in Christ Jesus. God loves our humanity and wants us to live it to the full because we are fantastic creations of God made to share God's life now and forever. O give thanks to the Lord for his love endures forever!

Each week, when I am at home, I meet with a group of very strong intelligent women whose lives are really centered on the Gospel and the presence of God. We have wide reaching conversations about many topics. They amaze me with their wisdom, their depth of understanding and their compassion. They have all suffered deeply in their lives but instead of that suffering making them bitter and inward looking it has done the opposite. I marvel sometimes at their openness to God and their desire to grow and change.

Just recently we were reflecting on the impact of culture on our lives and began to realise the invitation we have been given to stand apart from the systems of the day which influence us for better or for worse. We talked about the western world and the assumptions we have about material wealth and the presumptions we have about what it is that makes us appear successful. We came to the conclusion that much of it is superficial and shallow. So then we began to reflect on how much prayer and quiet time we need to free ourselves from believing the cultural norms of the day, and really take on the Gospel values that are eternal and which make us rejoice that we are human beings with an immense capacity to really live life to the full.

I often meet people who are full of hurt and anxiety about the past and in my book on forgiveness I tried to reflect on how much damage that can do to us as human beings. I often think of the amount of energy it takes to appear what we think is okay when it is anything but. To let go of our hurts and pain and lack of forgiveness and the masks we wear to cover them up is the greatest gift we can give ourselves and receive from God. It's when we start to let go of all that we carry around that we begin to discover the jewel that is humanity. Somehow we have to process what goes on within us or we simply blame, accuse, attack; or we become abusive control freaks forcing people to do what we want just to make ourselves feel better.

I came across this story a while back which illustrates the point. Someone had stolen the rabbi's bike. He felt sure that someone who worshipped at the synagogue must have taken it. So he decided to preach a sermon on the Ten Commandments. When he came to 'Thou shalt not steal', he made a great deal of the commandment, preaching beautifully about the scourge of theft and the collapse of standards in society. He used his bike as an illustration. However, when he came to the commandment, 'Thou shalt not commit adultery', he suddenly remembered where he had left his bike.

Another area that we probably have to let go in, is in the whole area of sexuality. Passion is not wrong; it is a wonderful gift from God who created us to feel it and know it. It is right that we should. I find it extraordinary the number of people who feel guilty in this area. To be passionate is very human. God created us as passionate, sexual beings. We have to rediscover that truth and let go of the false teachings that so many of us were given about sexuality. Sexuality is in many senses the energy of life and is much more than just sleeping with someone as the culture of the day would tell us.

I quoted earlier in the chapter from the book *Seeking Spirituality*. In the same book, Ronald Rolheiser defines sexuality as, '...a beautiful, good, extremely powerful sacred energy given us by God and experienced in every cell of our being as an irrepressible urge to overcome our incompleteness, to move towards unity with that which is beyond us.' To love anyone or anything passionately is simply an expression of that God-given reality. Rejoice in it, love it, accept it. Sure, we can make mistakes but we are sexual beings. We will love passionately; accept it, name it and let the anxiety about it go. Rejoice in who you are and what you are.

I think that as you enter into this process of letting go - and there is far more letting go needed in far more areas than just those I have shared about - we begin to discover the incredible truth that humanity is sacred. It is holy. God is enmeshed in the physical and intimately connected to us, not separate in any way. Therefore our humanity is sacred, holy, sanctified, blessed. Everything is stamped with the image of the creator. Just recently, Pope Francis said, 'I have a dogmatic certainty: God is in every person's life. God is in everyone's life. Even if the life of a person has been a disaster, even if it is destroyed by vices, drugs or anything else - God is in this person's life. You can - you must - try to seek God in every human life.'

That, of course, leads to an innate respect for every human person and a desire that every human person can rejoice in their humanity and see it as a gift from God. So we fight for justice and equality in every area that we can because of the extraordinary gift that we are to ourselves. That can make us extremely vulnerable, but maybe being vulnerable is at the heart of what it means to be human.

Recently, I came across this quotation from Brené Brown that I found quite challenging, 'Vulnerability is the birthplace of love, belonging, joy, courage, empathy, and creativity. It is the source of hope, empathy, accountability, and authenticity. If we want greater clarity in our purpose or deeper and more meaningful lives, vulnerability is the path.'

I remember the first time a man of the road put his arms around me and held me as he cried. His name was Patrick. I have written about him many times before because he had such a profound effect on me. He smelled and he was dirty. I felt so vulnerable but so alive. I can remember the first time I sat by the monument in Southport, the town I call my spiritual home, with the alcoholics and with them had to endure the hostile stares of people. It was an extraordinarily vulnerable place to be but the sharing that took place was amazing.

The challenge the Gospel gives us is to become a person who understands what humanity is about, who loves the world and everything in it. The challenge is to be vulnerable and compassionate and yet as Richard Rohr says, 'Vulnerability is not admired in our culture. If we have not touched and united with the vulnerable place within us, we are normally projecting seeming invulnerability outside and judging others for their weakness.'

So you have to own your inner life and embrace it and, in it, to meet the incarnate God who brings you life and who is enfleshed within us and amongst us. In it all, you will have eyes that see, not eyes that look. It is an invitation, already issued, to be in relationship with God, the world, with humanity, including ourselves.

The Gospels tell us very beautifully what it means to be real. Jesus told us so much about what humanity is really about, and all of it involves the challenge of letting go of what we thought it was about so that we could find again what it was really about.

We all want to be human and alive. Look deeply within yourself and begin to let go and you will begin to understand the gift that you are. I think that desire to be what we fully should be and to live a fully human life has been planted in our hearts by God, and is a wonderful gift as it impels us to explore and to discover.

So give thanks for the wonder of your being. Never stop journeying and discovering what it means to be a human being. Give thanks for the beauty of humanity. Give thanks for the immense amount of potential that lies within you. Give thanks for the emotional life, for the physical life and the spiritual life that is the person that you are. Rejoice and be glad.

# SIX

# GIVE THANKS FOR THE GIFT OF ONE ANOTHER

One of my saddest experiences was to visit an elderly lady. I had been asked to go and see her by her daughter who told me that her mum was suffering from depression. Maureen had agreed to see me because she had been to school with my mum and there was in her mind a connection, however tenuous.

She was in her eighties and on medication to try and help her anxiety levels. Maureen lived alone and was physically very healthy but emotionally quite poorly. Her daughter had told me that her mum was quite wealthy but that she refused to have any help in the house and spent much of her time alone. She would often tell her daughter not to come and visit because she did not want to see her. I went to her house and as soon as I arrived outside, everything spoke of neglect. The garden was out of control with trees and shrubs badly needing attention. It was so overgrown that from the front I was unable to see the front door or the ground floor windows. It seemed to be an old Victorian detached house and obviously had cellars and attics. The house had been built in a good part of town, but with paint peeling off and damaged windows, it looked almost derelict. I wondered what the neighbours thought about it.

I had been given a key to the back door because Maureen never responded to anyone knocking. I fought my way through brambles and foliage around the back of the house to find the door. Eventually I found it and I think I could have probably blown it open. I duly put the key in turned the rusty lock and found myself in a dirty, smelly kitchen.

I called out and was guided through the house by Maureen's voice. Everywhere was damp and decrepit. I remember thinking to myself if I lived there I would be badly depressed too! Eventually I found Maureen in a very big room. The curtains were drawn and it was gloomy and miserable as well as being dirty and filled with newspapers and half empty plates with congealed food on. It was obvious that she was not well at all and as soon as she saw me she began to weep. She was trying to apologise for the state of things and at the same time to tell me how bad she felt. It was awful.

The saddest part of our encounter was when she began to tell me how alone she was but that she did not want people around her. She hated company and really she just wanted to die. I stayed with her for some time and suggested at one point that we pray but she did not want to do that.

When eventually I left I could not help but be grateful for my own life and realised again something I have always known to be true. We need one another. We are made for relationship and I began to thank God for all the people in my life who make my life worth living. It seems to me that all too often we take one another for granted. I certainly do, and forget to thank God for the gift of those around me and at times even fail to give them the benefit of the doubt.

In the last chapter I reflected on the invitation to give thanks for the wonder of my being but I am also aware that I am not independent but interdependent. I am part of a great human chain. We depend on one another and bring life to one another. Therefore, as well as giving thanks for the wonder of my being, I should give thanks to God for the gift of others.

Throughout the Scriptures there is a growing awareness that without others in our lives we never really discover fully who we are. So others are as much a gift to us as we are to ourselves.

We first recognise this in the book of Genesis, when God creates 'the Human.' Scholars tell us that we should not understand this creation as an individual named Adam, although there are branches of Christianity that would insist on that. Rather, 'the Human' symbolises the whole of humanity. God is a loving creator and humanity is created from dust to share the life of the creator.

It is because of love that God breathes life into 'the Human' and it becomes a 'living being'. Humanity lives because Yahweh's breath is in it; when God's breath leaves, it dies. Every breath of every person depends directly upon God. It is amazing that we take our breath for granted and are often unaware that our very existence, our life depends on another.

Once the human is formed, God creates a place for humanity to live. We are told that God creates a garden which resembles a park with trees. Historians tell us that these park-like gardens were created by great kings in the ancient Near East. They were a source of shade from the sun and the kind of place where a king could relax. This is God's garden, and God uses it to walk with the human in the cool of the evening. The author mentions two trees that will function significantly in the development of humanity, the tree of life and the tree of the knowledge of good and evil, but that is another story.

The human is placed in the garden and given the task of looking after it. In ancient Near Eastern mythology, humanity is created to work for the gods so this is probably derived from that understanding.

Then we read of the creation of woman because 'It is not good for the human to be alone.' Right at the beginning we are made to be in relationship with others. God forms a woman from one of the ribs of 'the Human,' who one of the scholars says was put into a 'deep sleep' in case the act of creation is witnessed. The act of creation remains a mystery and always will. Suffice to know that we have a creator God who creates man and woman to be in relationship with one another. We are then told that the man calls his wife 'Eve,' a form of the Hebrew word for 'life,' and recognises that she will be the 'mother of all the living'. It has to be said that the creation of woman from man's rib does not in any way imply inferiority. Her mysterious creation by God from human substance simply reinforces connectivity relationship, the common nature she shares with man and the bond that unites them. She is his 'helper' implies that she is equal to, but other than, he is.

It is more or less certain that the accounts of creation are written by two distinct authors the Yahwist author and the Priestly author and the accounts are merged together to form what we have today in the book of Genesis. At the end of chapter two we are told that men and women are drawn to each other and marry. The terms 'leave' and 'cleave' are covenant terms and suggest that marriage is here viewed as a covenantal relationship. The Yahwist account of creation is much more limited than the Priestly account; it is concerned with the human relationship to the soil and the relationship between man and woman, not with the creation of a universe; but for our purposes, it is very clear that we are made for relationship and it is in relationship that we find ourselves. So it is right to be grateful and to give thanks for others in our lives.

As the Scriptural understanding of God and humanity develops we eventually arrive at the Song of Songs that wonderful earthy sexual reflection on humanity and relationship. It is a love-song of haunting beauty with outrageous imagery and huge excesses; it was meant to be sung as a celebration of love, beauty and intimacy. The Song found its early popularity within the social and religious life of ancient Israel. It was most probably sung as entertainment at local celebrations of the various harvest festivals, accompanied by dancing at a village wedding, sung as court entertainment at the royal palace in Jerusalem, or at happy family reunions or gatherings.

Even the rabbis of the first century AD recognised its popular nature as a song even if not everyone approved of it. Rabbi Akiva who lived in the 1st century and was a great authority on Jewish tradition wrote, 'He who rills his voice in the chanting of the Song of Songs in the banquet halls and treats it as a secular song has no share in the world to come.' So the Song was poetry meant for musical recital.

In listening to the Song, we find that it is speaking not only to us, but about us, and I have to say when I read it, I find myself drawn into the movement of the verses and the atmosphere that it creates. One of the authors that I have read in the past said 'Our imaginations are stimulated and we begin to identify with the lovers on their journey of love, of self-discovery and of fulfilment.' The Song of Songs goes a long way with its imagery and its sheer joy of sexuality to remind us that it is all gift and that we should rejoice in it. It is the bible's antidote to shame and narrowness in its exuberance and its desire that we live life to the full. So we should give thanks for the gift of sexuality and attraction, all of it God given and something to be grateful for within ourselves and within others.

As the Scriptures move on, it seems that our relationship with one another is to be characterised by love. The prophets will spend a lot of time reflecting on the call to love. Hosea is to love his wife even when she prostitutes herself. Isaiah reminds us that we must look after the widow and the orphan. Amos tells us that we must treat the poor and the broken as though they were our own.

When we get to the Gospels, Jesus' greatest commandment seems to be that we love one another. Why? It is because we are made to be in right relationship with one another and any form of abuse or rejection of others is not part of God's plan for humanity. In John's Gospel particularly, there is an emphasis on relation-ship with love at the core. Chapter fifteen is all about communion. It is about what it means to be present to another, to remain with another; it speaks of friendship, real friendship, that mutual indwelling that has been focused on throughout the Gospel. It invites us to take the risk of intimacy, of knowing and being known, of being vulnerable and weak with someone else, if you are to know how to be a friend. Somehow, in entering into that sort of relationship with another person, you will experience that sort of relationship with God. The whole of the Chapter is captured in the phrase, 'What I command you is to love one another'. It is an invitation to be constantly calling on his life, love, forgiveness, peace, so that we can be seen to stand in the name of Jesus as a sign of love through the relationships that we have. The human qualities of love and compassion for the other brings us life and is something to be grateful for. It is also true to say that compassion, mercy and love that comes from others should also make us grateful for the gift of the other.

Back in the 1990's I broke down. It was because of the pressure I felt in trying to do what I thought the perfect Priest should do. It was because of my early childhood and the effects of my dad's alcoholism, huge family financial crises and the death of my mum who had always been the one constant in my life. I was university chaplain at the time which was very pressurised, and it all just got too much and I broke inside. I went to a therapist for whom I am now very grateful, as she led me through the pain and the brokenness. I was very much aware of the love that sustained me in my friends in very real, practical ways as they sat with me when I could not speak, fed me when I was unable to think about food and dragged me out to places when all I wanted was to be alone in the misery. In our community we have a phrase that has always meant a lot to us: 'None of us have it all together but all together we have it all.' I experienced the truth of that during that period in my life and I will be ever grateful for the gift of others who drew me back to life through loving compassion and the odd beer or two!

One of the major themes in John's first letter is that of love. God is love and so we must love one another. The author insists that our belief and our behaviour go together. If we love God then we will obey God's commands. If we obey God's commands then we will love our brothers and sisters. What we believe in our hearts will be expressed by our lives that love is the only way. The author of the first letter tells us that we can be sure we know God if we obey God's commands. This does not mean living by a rigid code of laws. It means falling in love with humanity and discovering a God who has first loved us. It is about loving in response to love. So give thanks for the gift of others who bring the challenge of love to the fore.

It is true that love of others was right at the heart of the Jewish Torah. However this is a new commandment because Jesus has shown the kind of love involved. He has washed his disciples' feet, acting as their slave even though he is their Lord. We are to love our brothers and sisters; that includes every human person who walks this earth. Jesus has shown us how to love by laying down his life. This kind of loving is intensely practical. It means sharing what we have. It means giving to those in need. It means not just good ideas and holy thoughts, but action. We are very good at the holy thoughts but not always the action!

The heart of all truth is that God is love. Love is not something God has created, but the very essence of who God is. God can only love. Anyone who shows God's self giving love is reflecting God for the world. That means that God operates outside the parameters that we so often put on God. God is being made present wherever there is love. Such love is 'made complete', as John says in one of his letters, when it comes from God through us and brings life to others.

The quality of all our relationships, with family, church, neighbours and strangers, is a sign of our relationship with God. It is very likely that if we are in a bad relationship with someone else, we are also in a bad relationship with God. The way we treat one another is the way we treat God. That is not a very comfortable thought but it is the truth if we believe in the mystery of incarnation and the presence of God in each human person. Give thanks for the mystery of community and for the presence of God in our midst.

Several years ago I led a Parish mission in one of our poorer areas. As a team we went in with all our 'stuff' - music, song, story, visuals; but that community taught me more about love and life and being grateful for those around us than I have learnt in other, more salubrious, places. During the coffee break, one elderly lady took me on one side and nodded towards another lady. 'See her', she said, 'every Sunday when I come to mass she smiles and nods at me and I do the same back but I never really knew her. Six months ago I had to have chemotherapy and I do not have any family and was at the end of my tether wondering how I would manage. One day there was a knock on the door and she was there with a bit of scouse in a dish. She brought me my dinner every night for three months.' She then looked over at another woman and said, 'she did the washing' and then at a man, 'he walked the dog'. People she hardly knew reached into her life and touched it. When I asked her how she felt about all these people she started to cry and said that she was so very grateful for them. I heard countless stories like that throughout the week and by the end of it, I felt grateful for the gift of others.

One of the keystones of St Paul's theology is that of unity or community. It is not, for Paul, a religion of practices, the way it became, but much more of participation and therefore radical transformation into an organic unity in Christ. We are his body. The relationships between us are deeper and far more real than even our blood ties. They are spiritual bonds that tie us together and which can never be broken. Surely we can only thank God for this.

All Paul's ethics were tied up with his concept of community. In his writings, he has lists of vices and virtues that encourage people living some sort of social, communal, forgiving life together. The sins of rivalry, jealousy, greed that make you an individual, make it impossible for you to live in community. Co-operation, unity, forgiveness, patience, mercy are his values. Everything is based on his understanding of people living in unity and communion together.

As I have written before it is a cause of great sadness to me that we are born into a period of history which is probably the most individualistic culture the world has ever produced. Everything is about me and my fulfilment. Paul is coming from a different place. He sees everything in terms of community. He knows the truth of the body of Christ.

I often wonder whether we understand at all what Paul is talking about when we can live in a world where so many people are starving and living below the poverty line. I wonder, do we have that sense of being part of one another and how grateful we are for that truth? Of course, it brings its challenges as the desire for justice and peace then has to be at the very core of our being. For Paul we are, as community, the living presence of Christ in the world and as such, like the Lord before us, we are to be love for the world; not just do loving things but become love. Somebody once said to me that the litmus test for our Christianity is how we respond to the least of our brothers and sisters.

However, maybe it goes even deeper. Are we aware that everything we do has an impact on the body? Even the things we

do in secret. Our actions and thoughts influence the way we
relate to others and think about others even when we think
nobody else knows about them. If you harbour unforgiveness, it
will make you hard hearted. If you are judgemental, even deep
within, you will not be as compassionate as you could be. If you
are doing things that make you ashamed, the guilt and shame
you feel will affect the way you relate to others. The list goes on
and on. John Donne's words 'no man is an island' ring true when
thinking about the body of Christ.

Thank goodness we have been given the power of God to enable
us to become what we are called to be. Always ask the spirit to
help you understand that we are the body of Christ, and pray
that we might all be free to live out our calling in the world.

I have been part of a Christian community for many years and,
as I look back, I know that I have found myself through the
people with whom I have shared my life. I thank God for the
simple relationships that make life worth living. I thank God for
the community house where some of us lived together for many
years. I remember the Agape magazine that we printed for several
years, the days where we gathered people together and the
conferences we organised and I give thanks. I thank God for the
holidays and pilgrimages that have taken place over the years.

We have been privileged to share with amazing people: Cardinal
Suenens, Richard Rohr and Ian Petit to name just a few, and the
list goes on. We give thanks for the way in which many people
have worked together recording conferences. It is good to

remember the homeless project and the Sandymount project which helped people explore spirituality in a safe place. It is right to give thanks for it all. It has been a huge part of my life for over thirty years and I am very grateful that God brought me into that community.

As I write, Matthew's Gospel comes to mind. Matthew constantly invites us to enter into a new social order. He invites us to turn our way of thinking upside down and to live in a radically different way. It is that new way of thinking that is central to any Christian community. Emmaus, the name of our community, only exists because God has touched our lives and made us see differently. The challenge of that new way of living goes on for us today. If we are not learning to forgive, learning to serve, learning to go the extra mile and to always give one another the benefit of the doubt, then we are a million miles removed from the Gospel. If we are not prepared to put up with the mistakes of others and to try and deal with our hurts rather than stand on our own dignity, we have not understood the Gospel of Christ.

Matthew gives us the sermon on the Mount and says to us, 'Blessed are the poor'; and then he goes on to say to us, 'Love your enemies, forgive those who hurt you, always be the ones to make the first move whether it is your fault or not.' It is an invitation to be open and vulnerable and available. It is a new way of thinking, a completely different understanding than the prevailing culture, which would have us defend ourselves, possess more and more, hold grudges and get our own back.

I often think Matthew's Gospel is a lesson for those of us who think that following Jesus is about the things we do in Church. Matthew was telling a very legalistic community that following the Lord has far more to do with our lifestyles, our attitudes, our relationships, and what goes on deep within us, than it has to do with worshipping God. Our worship is to make us more aware of the presence of God in us and in each other and so to give thanks.

In our community we have walked with one another down the years and at times we have hurt one another. We are still together because the Gospel is always challenging us to stay together and live that radical new life that challenges the world. We are still having gatherings, and are always inviting people to come together to experience God. We are still recording conferences to get the Gospel message to as wide an audience as we can. We still have links with homeless projects and ecumenical initiatives. God is not finished with Emmaus yet. What the next years will bring only God knows, but I guess we look to the future knowing that God will be with us and that there is always more.

For the purposes of this chapter, all we have done and lived out is because God showed us how important it is to recognise that we are called into relationship and to give thanks for that calling. So I would encourage you to be filled with gratitude for those around you and the impact that they have in your life. Give thanks to God each day for the gift of a communal life and pray for the strength to live out that life in wonder and gratitude.

# SEVEN

# GIVE THANKS FOR THE WORD

Many years ago, I was at a conference led by Frances Hogan, an Irish woman who has a profound love of the Scriptures and a wonderful ability to interpret them for others. It was the first time I had met this woman and it was she who began to open my heart to the Scriptures. I was about fifteen at the time and did not know one end of the Bible from another, but I did want to know Jesus and so I felt within me a real pull towards the Scriptures. I drank in every word that she said as though I were in a desert and being offered cool refreshing water. I remember one phrase she said which made a deep impression on me and helped me to understand how important the Word of God is for us. She said, quoting St. Jerome, 'Ignorance of Scripture is ignorance of Jesus.' Since then I suppose I have spent a lot of time reflecting on the Scriptures and thanking God for the gift that they are.

I was not always very happy when I was at the seminary. Much of what I was taught seemed irrelevant to me. I also found some of the traditions and the seminary lifestyle difficult to handle. I had been catapulted into a profound experience of God some years earlier. For me it was hard to equate what went on in the seminary with my experience of a God who brought extraordinary life. Much of what I experienced was less than life giving. The one thing I did love were the lectures and courses about the Scriptures and again I drank in every word, loving the scholarship and the reflective aspects of the lectures. I was lucky enough to be taught in the main by priests who had made the Scriptures their life, and that shone through as they shared with us. So I often thank God for the light the Scriptures were in a difficult time in my life.

What I began to believe with all my heart in those early days of my faith journey was this. These Scriptures are the word of God, inspired by the Spirit, written by communities of faith to help others on their faith journey, and that God speaks to his people through them. I both experienced that and heard it said time and time again. When I went to the Seminary I discovered that belief is in keeping with the teaching of the church and particularly that which is found in the Vatican Document *Dei Verbum.*

So this Word is power! We are not just reading old stories. We are discovering God's way of communicating God's presence. We are being invited into a dance of love with God in the same way those ancient people entered into a dance of love with God. What do I mean by presence? Well I guess it is that indescribable sense of relationship, where we know by faith that another is walking with us and addressing us and entering into the reality of our lives.

The documents of the Church remind us that God is as really present in the word we hear as in the Eucharist we receive. Yet, in my Catholic tradition it is unusual to find people who listen, who read it voraciously and, if we are going to be honest, allow it to be a living force in our lives. This is God speaking to us and feeding us and yet, in the Catholic tradition, if we were faced with a service of the word each morning instead of Mass most of us would not go. We would want to receive communion. Yet the truth is we are fed at the table of the word and the Eucharist and both are as important as each other. I do not know about you but I was brought up believing in the need to be really reverent when in the presence of the Eucharist, and that is right and good. However I was never aware that the same God was present in the Word or that the same God was present in my brothers and sisters.

So what can this living word do for us? I think first of all it can enable us to discover the reality of who God is. We meet Jesus, the face of God, and are opened up to relationship with that God. Secondly, it tells our story, our faith story, the difficulties we have in life, the challenges we have to face, the big questions that we wrestle with. The Scriptures reveal the universal patterns of human experience. You know, the questions that are asked today in the face of great tragedy, illness and sadness, are the same questions that someone dying in first century Palestine would have asked. Thirdly they challenge us in the way we relate to one another and see one another. Dare we believe that God is present in another human person, and if we do, what does that mean?

When we enter into that sort of understanding of the word of God, we find that it is always new because it is always leading us more deeply into the mystery of God and the mystery of humanity. We will find it calling us ever more deeply into a faith relationship with God, trusting and believing that ultimately all will be well because of the presence of God. I know in my heart that the Bible is a love story between God and God's people. I was in a Parish recently sharing that the love of God is like a never-ending fountain gushing from the heart of God. It is about the way in which we surrender to that extraordinary love. At the heart of the Bible is a God who is love, can only love and who will go to any lengths for us because of love.

As I have reflected on the Scriptures over the years, I have become more and more aware of just how powerful they are and the effect they can have on our lives. I was recently listening to some talks given by Fr Raniero Cantalamessa; for many years he has been the preacher to the Papal household. He was saying that the Word of God is a living extension of God himself and getting in touch with the Word of God is getting in touch with God. It is nice to have what I have written confirmed by the Papal preacher! Whenever we read the Scriptures we meet the living God. That is an incredible gift and something to rejoice in constantly. When we read the Scriptures we are encountering the living God, the God of Moses, Isaac and Jacob. The God of the living, not the dead, is the one we meet. If we are supposed to encounter the living God in the Scriptures then that must have an effect on us, and if it does not, then it can only be that somehow we are not as open as we maybe thought we were.

I am absolutely certain that one of the reasons why the Scriptures do not always have an effect on our lives is because we ask the wrong questions of them. We get very hung up on whether or not the Scriptures are historically true. Did Adam and Eve exist? Did the miracles happen? The vast majority of the Scriptures is based on oral tradition and is theology rather than chronology so those sorts of questions are not as important as we think. The people who wrote the Bible do not have the sense of truth and the sense of history that we have. The remembrance of the event is not to tell you what happened but the meaning of what happened. It is always important for the reader of the Word to ask the questions, 'What did the writers mean? What is it saying to us about life and relationship? What is it saying to us about the world and our role in it?' It is so that you can find meaning. That is what can be called the Hebrew sense of history, or the Hebrew sense of truth, which is the sense of truth of almost all primitive peoples and a much deeper sense of truth than our purely factual, 'Did it or did it not happen?' Meaning tells you the truth. Truth is not about physical space or chronological time.

If you are asking the wrong questions of the Scriptures, then you will not allow them to penetrate any further than your minds. Do not get hung up on whether or not things happened or did not happen. That is a secondary problem, and as soon as it becomes a primary one, you have lost the battle and the Scriptures will only ever remain at the level of head knowledge. We will never encounter the living God. What is really important are the questions, 'Can God happen now?' 'Can life happen now?' 'Can the Kingdom happen now?' 'Is it happening now?' 'How does it happen?' It is when we can answer those questions that

we will encounter God and be filled with gladness at the gift of
the Word. You see, what really matters is that we have a present
moment encounter with God so we experience in the here and
now his presence, the building of the kingdom, the life-giving
movement of his Spirit. That encounter can happen through
reading and praying through the Word of God and can fill us
with joy.

So some other questions that I would ask you to consider are
these: 'Are you longing for economic, physical and spiritual
liberation? Do you need a Saviour? Is your heart burning within
you with a desire for freedom?' If you can answer, Yes, then
maybe the Scriptures will begin to work their miracle on you.
Maybe you will have an encounter with God through ancient
stories, traditions and symbols. If you answer, No, then maybe
all they will ever be is a book that 'churchy' people read and say
this is the Word of God.

Years ago I met a religious sister called Barbara. She had
multiple sclerosis. Her condition affected her speech and her
mobility. She was one the freest, most wonderful people I have
ever met. Her eyes sparkled with a deep inner joy. Her heart
brimmed over with love and even when she was tired she had
room for people in her life, particularly the poor and the broken.
She told me that when she had received her diagnosis she was
plunged into a deep depression. She had not been a sister for
very long and had been full of what she was going to do for God
and all of it, it seemed to her, was taken away in one fell swoop
in the doctor's words, 'You have multiple sclerosis'.

At that time in her life, Barbara's prayer was to pray the divine office in community and to go to chapel for meditation. She heard the Scriptures at Mass but never thought of reading them at any other time. In the midst of this depression, with her body beginning to fail, she cried out to God, 'Help me'. She told me that she heard an audible voice speaking, so much so that she looked around to see who was in the chapel. There was no one. Again she cried out to God and again she heard the voice. The words spoken were simple: 'Read my Word'. She decided that, even if she was going crazy and hearing voices, she would do what she had heard. She began to read the word of God. She read commentaries on the word and she prayed it through. As the months went by Barbara realised that she was changing within. Her depression lifted. She began to see people rather than hide away. In time, she became the woman I met, full of life and love and a wonderful gift to me. The Word had become her life support and no longer empty words read at Church on Sundays.

Barbara's experience tells us what will happen if we do begin to recognise that this Word really is leading us into the presence of God. It tells us what will happen if we do ask the right questions of it. It helps us understand what will happen if we do recognise in the depths of our being that we need liberation. I mentioned earlier in this chapter the series of talks by Fr Raniero Cantalamessa. In them he was saying that the purpose of the bible is threefold. Firstly, we will grow in knowledge of God. Secondly, we will grow in awareness of ourselves and that awareness can set us free, Thirdly, we will be forced into action.

It is obvious that the word has to be acted on or it simply remains at the level of head knowledge.

So firstly, what is the Spirit saying to us about God? Throughout the Old or First Testament we read the story of a people who are growing in awareness of who God is. What we discover is that God is a God of love who is on the side of those in need. We find that God is a God very much identified with the human situation that God is with his people. We have already reflected on the image of God that the First Testament can seem to present earlier in this book. That is where it is important to ask the right questions. The question to ask all the time is, 'What does it mean? What truth is it telling us? I really believe that the truth it is telling us lies behind the stories and the images used and the Spirit wants to reveal that truth to us. The Scriptures will enable us to discover who God is if we give them the space and the time. In the New or Second Testament we discover in and through the life of Jesus that God is in the business of setting us free. We are so loved that God wants us to be free of anything that stops us knowing who God is.

That invitation to freedom was costly, and so we find Jesus giving his life for the sake of real freedom. His call to freedom was too powerful for the world to take. The Jewish leaders were not able to cope with his threat to their systems and their traditions, so they nailed him to the cross; but you cannot kill love and so it burst forth, raising Jesus to new life and giving us access to a love that can change the world. That is who God is for us, pure unconditional love that will go to any lengths for you and me. If the Scriptures reveal that to us, then I think we will be filled with a joy and gratitude that knows no bounds.

Val and Joan are two women who come to our house for the short courses on the Scriptures that we run. They are ordinary women. Val is a widow and Joan married. They live in the same street and have been friends for a long time. They have been stalwarts of their local parish, always trying to put events on and encouraging others to come along. The reason for their lives of service is because, as they have reflected on the Scriptures, they have discovered much of the reality of the love of God and it has filled them with a deep joy. They both want others to know what they have discovered. At times in their lives, both of them have suffered. They have been anxious about their families and their children, but this sense of the love of God has filled them to overflowing. They have begun to discover the love of God and it has changed their lives.

The second action of the Spirit through the Scriptures is to help us grow in knowledge of ourselves. The key to all spiritual growth is self-knowledge and self-awareness. We need to spend a lot of time reflecting on who we are and what there is within us that needs to be touched by the power of God. In Paul's letter to the Ephesians, we are invited to grow strong in our innermost self. Reflecting on the Scriptures and what they teach us about humanity will enable us to do that.

In John's Gospel, there is only one sin that condemns and that sin is in not knowing who you are in the sight of God. It is not knowing that you are a child of God and that God is your father. Not to believe in who you are is to live in self-doubt, anxiety, and hatred, and that is sheer hell. Not to listen to the voice that says you are of ultimate value is to condemn ourselves to a life that is less than God wants for us. So how do we begin to believe who we are in the sight of God? How do we begin to hear the voice above all other voices which tells us that we are worthwhile? It seems to me that the answer lies in the journey of self-acceptance which results in peace. It lies in knowing that God is happy with us as we are, but at the same time, is calling us to growth and movement.

The call to become fully human is very much at the centre of the Gospels. I do not know if you have read the passage at the beginning of the Acts of the Apostles where the disciples stand looking up into the sky after Jesus had been taken from them. An angel appears and says to them, 'Why are you Galileans standing looking up into the sky?' Well, I think we spend an awful lot of time super-spiritualising everything and not realising the wonderful call that the Gospel gives us to discover what it means to be human. We stand looking up into the sky instead of discovering what life is about; waiting for Jesus to come in from the outside when he is already there on the inside, waiting to be discovered.

If you meet Jesus he will challenge you to become the person that you were created to be. He will invite you to recognise the goodness that is in yourself and to love yourself. He will invite you to recognise and share your emotions and feelings. He will invite you to own your inner life and embrace it. He will show you how to fall in love with yourself and as you fall in love with yourself you will discover that the very things within you that frightened you are the very things that help you be fully human. Your fragility, your vulnerability, your pain are the things that make you alive if you only learn to face them and thank God for them.

Life is about discovering the beauty of what we are. It is about becoming real and comfortable with every aspect of ourselves. Francis of Assisi said that it is about embracing the leper within ourselves and finding that he turns out to be a prince instead. So the Spirit wants to work a miracle in us through the Scriptures to enable us to be the most fully human people it is possible for us to be. So give thanks for the power of the word that can take us to that place.

Fourteen years ago I met Mick who was an Irish man who had been living here in England for more than thirty years. It was on a retreat that I was leading and Mick came to have a chat with me one day. He told me that he had had a very difficult childhood in Dublin. He was illegitimate and had been given up for adoption as a baby, but adoption had never taken place and he was left in a children's home. He said it was neither good nor bad but that there was very little compassion or love in the place. He told me that, as he grew up, he became more and more hard. He was determined to make his way in the world and earn lots of money and he did not care who he hurt on the way - and hurt people he did. His wife and two children were casualties of the bitterness and anger that he had built up in himself. He had been divorced for several years. He had cheated on business associates and did some dodgy work in the building trade. He earned lots of money but eventually his dodgy work caught up with him. He was arrested, taken to court and sent to jail for twelve months. It was while he was there that the Prison Chaplain ran a course on the Bible that would change Mick for ever. As he prayed and studied the Scriptures he realised how inhuman he had become. He began to ask God to free him and make him less cold and hard. He began to hear the call to be loving, compassionate and forgiving and as the months went by, he told me that he changed slowly. When he got out of prison he set about undoing the damage that he had done as best he could, and when I met him he was a lovely warm, free, Irishman. The third action of the Spirit through the Scriptures is to send us out to proclaim the truth and beauty of God's presence to the world. What we have received we are to share. I used to have contact with a large youth group in the North East of England called Emmanuel, and the priest who was involved with them would always say, 'You have heard the Word of God, now go and do it.'

You might be asking yourself what you are to do. It is very simple... share the message of love that you have received. Share the reality of God's love for you. Share the life-giving message of liberation that the Scriptures give you, not necessarily through what you say but always through what you are and what you do. Richard Rohr says you can only talk about a journey if you are on the journey. You will only share the Good News with people if you allow the Good News to happen within you.

Talk about the God you have met in the Scriptures. Talk about the God you meet daily. Live your life as though you really are being liberated. Be honest and open about who you are and what you are. Listen, and be compassionate to those around you because you have heard the Spirit whispering His word of compassion in your ear. Accept and tolerate difference. Do not presume all the time that you have it right and those who think differently than you have it wrong.

I encountered an incredible woman when I was a Parish priest in Southport. Her name was Aggie and although I had known her for many years, I did not know her well. I was looking for someone to clean the house and a friend of mine suggested Aggie who did a bit of cleaning around the town. Aggie came and stayed for the five years I spent there. What was incredible about her, as well as her sense of humour and fun, was the way she reached out to the poor, the disadvantaged, the broken and the needy. She was a powerhouse when, as a Parish community, we decided to reach out to those who live on the edges. Aggie would spend hours talking to landlords, finding furniture and clothes, and producing food. She told me one day that it was the Gospel passage from Matthew twenty-five that inspired her. She said when she realised that what she did for the least of these she did for Christ, her life was turned upside down. The word of God had struck home. Aggie died at a relatively young age and at her funeral, I had a sense of the Lord saying to her, 'Well done good and faithful servant'.

So why give thanks for the Word of God? Because of what the

Spirit is doing through the Scriptures. The Spirit is inviting you to move deeper into the person of God. You are being called into intimacy with the God of Universe. You are challenged to move more deeply into yourself, to understand yourself, to grow in your innermost being, to become all that you were created to be. You are invited to proclaim the truth of God to the world, a truth that you have experienced and which has given you life. So desire liberation with all your heart. Bring that desire to God, ask the right questions of the Scriptures and see what will happen as you journey, always giving thanks for the Word of God.

# EIGHT

# GIVE THANKS FOR
# THE GIFT OF HOPE

S ome years ago, a second cousin of mine rang me to tell me that she had been going through some of her mother's belongings. In a trunk in the attic she had found some letters written by her mother's grandparents, who were my great grandparents. John and Mary Lloyd were born in the 1850's near Chester. My dad's cousin, Bettie, remembered her grandmother who died in 1927 as a cheerful, bright woman who looked after those less fortunate than herself. John and Mary were born into poverty but through hard work had eventually become pub landlords. Both of them taught themselves to read and write, hence the letters found in a trunk in Abergele in the 1990's.

They had been written when John Lloyd who, for a while, was in the army, fighting in the Boer war. The Second Boer War was fought between the British Empire and two Boer states, the South African Republic and the Orange Free State, over the British Empire's influence in South Africa between October 1899 and May 1902.

When I heard of the find, I went across to my cousin's house to look at these letters. They were extraordinarily fragile and very difficult to read but the letters were filled with love, one for another and full of details of life as they knew it. From John, there was talk of the camps, and the men he shared his life with and the weather and the flies. From Mary, details of their children's lives and the ordinary day-to-day existence in Victorian England. What struck me at the time was how filled with hope they were. They looked to the future when peace would most surely come and they were filled with anticipation and certainty that, whatever the future held, it would be good because God was good.

Whenever I reflect on hope I find myself asking the question, 'what is it?' I know that without hope, life is empty but I have discovered that sometimes it is easier to say what hope is not rather than what it is. The American Franciscan Richard Rohr says, 'Hope is not occasioned by things working out as we expected. If our hope rises or falls according to circumstances, we do not have hope. As Paul says so well in Romans, 'we can be happy right now. Our trials produce endurance, and endurance produces a stubborn hope, a hope that will not disappoint us. It is the love of God poured forth in our heart'.'

So hope is not dependent on the circumstances of our lives or whether people like us or do not like us. Hope is not wishful thinking like, 'I hope I win the lottery' or 'I hope Liverpool win the league'. Nor is hope optimism. The great spiritual writer Henri Nouwen when reflecting on hope and optimism, saw them as being completely differing attitudes. Optimism is the expectation that life and the things that make up life, even mundane things like the weather, will get better despite evidence to the contrary. I think it is characterised in the wonderful Dickens personality, Mr. Micawber. Hope, on the other hand, seems to be the willingness to believe in the certainty that God will fulfil God's promises to us in a way that leads us to true freedom. If you are a person of hope you will live in the moment with the knowledge and trust that the future and all it might bring is in God's hands. This means that all will be well despite the circumstances we might find ourselves in. Hope has a certainty that mere optimism can never have.

Nouwen writes, 'All the great spiritual leaders in history were people of hope. Abraham, Moses, Ruth, Mary, Jesus, Rumi, Gandhi, and Dorothy Day all lived with a promise in their hearts that guided them toward the future without the need to know exactly what it would look like. Let us live with hope.'

For those of us who are of the Christian faith, hope is a person who was longed for and waited for. If you go to the Scriptures you will find right at the centre of Jewish belief a growing awareness and hope that God was coming to save them. The prophets in particular began to see that only God could save them from being the whipping boys of the Middle East. That led them to a broad understanding of salvation. They had the vision of the goal. They understood the end. The Jewish tradition was unique. The revelation of God meant that for them history was going somewhere. It had meaning and significance. It was heading in a direction and God's word was leading it in a direction. The Jews were an eschatological people. Eschaton is a Greek word that means the last things. It points towards the final goal and so the prophets, despite some of their gloomy proclamations, lived in hope because of the big picture that they saw. Isaiah,

Jeremiah, Hosea, Amos and others, were all able to see beyond the mess of Israel's situation and be filled with hope in the goodness of God, and somehow to know the truth that God would not be defeated.

That going somewhere, that direction and purpose, is part of our story too. When we know that life has purpose, it frees us from being narrowed into the present moment and thinking there is nothing else. It is good to live in the present moment, and I have preached on it often enough, but the call is to recognise too, that there is always more. So often we forget where we come from and we do not see where we are going, and of course that can minimise our hope. If we do not believe that we come from God and will go to God and that the whole world is struggling towards that, why would we hope? Many years ago, I was sitting on a coach in Austria and the guide was telling a story about a Goblin who lived on the mountain that we were going to, and this Goblin had the ability to grant people long lives, up to nine hundred and ninety nine years. As the guide was saying it, a friend of mine looked around and said, 'Is that all? I am going to live for ever.' It was said tongue in cheek, but it came from a deep hope in the presence of God in whom life has direction and purpose.

I think we have to become an eschatological people. That means we need to hear the message proclaimed by the prophets. We need to be freed from our preoccupation that the present is all there is if we are to live in hope. The prophetic writings free us to stand in the midst of the world filled with hope. When we are freed and filled with hope we will then be able to say how good it is to live in this world. It is then that we will give thanks for the hope that fills our hearts.

So, hoping was a way of life for the people of Israel. The sadness is that they were not open enough to see their hopes fulfilled. They did not expect their hope to be fulfilled in a tiny baby born in a hovel, who grow up to be a radical preacher who questioned every system they had created for themselves. Nor did they expect their hope to be a man who made himself unclean by touching those who were outside the temple system, and who eventually died a criminal's death on a rubbish heap called Golgotha.

Pope Francis has recently said, 'But hope is something else. It is not optimism. Hope is a present, it is a gift from the Holy Spirit and that is why Paul says: 'never disappoint yourself'- hope never lets you down. Why? Because it is a gift from the Holy Spirit but Paul tells us that hope has a name. Hope is Christ. We cannot say: 'I have hope in God', No' if you do not say: 'I have hope in Jesus Christ, a person that is alive. That is not hope; it could be good mood optimism. Jesus the hope renews everything. It is a constant miracle.'

Hope has a name, and I guess the question for all of us to ask ourselves is whether or not our hope lies in Christ or if it lies elsewhere. It is of course fine to hope in Christ when everything is going well. Of course, our hope is in God then. However, I often think that the challenge for all of us is to hope in God in the darkest moments, to hope in God in the moments of questioning, and wondering, and doubting. It is to hope in God when it looks as though our worlds are falling apart, and sometimes to trust that God's ways are not our ways. Our hope in God has nothing to with life's circumstances but everything to do with the bigger picture. God can still be our hope when the world is falling apart because God is God and our future in God is assured whatever our passing circumstances may be. I came across this definition by John Piper who is a Baptist Minister, 'Christian hope is when God has promised that something is going to happen and you put your trust in that promise. Christian hope is a confidence that something will come to pass because God has promised it will come to pass.' We may never see the outcome of our hope but it can illuminate our lives.

I think I learnt that lesson early on in life from Mrs Doyle. She used to come to our flat to clean. We had nothing, but Mrs Doyle had less than we had, and what we had was always shared. So Mrs Doyle, who was a proud woman, would not accept charity but would come and clean. My Mum would give her a shepherd's pie or a pan of scouse in 'payment' for her work. She was a real Mrs Malaprop and my memories of the things she said often make me laugh. I remember her telling my mum that she was sorry for breaking her pelvis. She meant the pelmet that held up the curtains! She often complained about the condemnation that ran down the windows in our damp flat. However she was a good soul who was part of the framework of my early life.

Mrs Doyle had lived in the centre of town and like many people in Liverpool had been moved into the suburbs after the second world war because of the devastation caused by the bombing. Whole communities saw their way of life torn apart as they were moved into new areas around the city. Mrs Doyle lived in a maisonette with a brood of children and, as far as I remember, no Mr Doyle. Her life was hard. She lived hand to mouth and her children were scruffy, dressed in rags and hand me downs. Yet she was one of the most wonderful faith-filled people I have ever met. Looking back, her unshakeable hope in God had a profound influence on me as she sang hymns while she cleaned. I often wondered what she had to sing about. From her earliest days, she had been steeped in faith. Her mother had taken her to church in town. She had taught her novenas and devotions, which are a very traditional way of praying in the Catholic world.

All of this had stood her in good stead as she learned from an early age that God could be trusted. This meant that, despite the circumstances of her life she was always filled with hope in the goodness of God. Her conversation was punctuated with thanks to God for all her blessings. While she worried about her children and their future, ultimately her hope was always in God. I have always loved the story of the Samaritan woman that we find in chapter four of John's Gospel. It is a story of rekindled hope. A woman goes to a well to draw water in the hottest part of the day when the well would be empty, or so she thought. What she did not know was that this was to be her day! In the middle of a complicated, difficult, messy life, Jesus was going to quench her thirst with life-giving water. He was going to give her hope. When our hearts are open and honest, he will quench

our thirst and fill us with hope too. I guess that is what I saw in
Mrs Doyle - an open honest heart that had been filled with hope
in God.

As she drew near to the well, the woman saw a man standing
there. She probably did not intend to get too close because she
knew by the way he was dressed that he was not a Samaritan. I
guess her plan was to help herself to the usual supply of water
and move on quickly before she was insulted verbally, or worse
things happened to her. She was shocked when the man spoke
to her. However, more than shocked, she seems both embarrassed and scared. She covers it all with a show of wit and
aggression.

His request is very surprising to her. He asks her for a drink.
That seems simple enough, on the face of it, until you remember
that he is a Jew, and Jews and Samaritans do not mix with one
another. The request for a drink throws her into confusion as
she recognises this stranger as different. He is not a typical Jew,
ready to dismiss her with a quick insult or worse.

I often ask myself, what it is that brings us human beings to the
well in the desert? I have reached the conclusion that, whatever
it is, we might find ourselves unexpectedly disturbed, like
the woman in the story. As we face the reality within, we will
be challenged to move out of our comfort zones, our lack of
forgiveness, our hurts. Jesus can disrupt everything we have been
comfortable with. That disturbance is something that is difficult
to handle, but usually, when it happens, we end up being filled

with hope in the goodness of God. The Samaritan woman, despite feeling uncomfortable, does not run away. She stays and enters a life-giving experience. Jesus gives her the opportunity and the hope to be who she was created to be, a beloved child of God.

Pope Francis reminds us: 'Jesus, the hope, renews everything. So hope is a constant miracle. The miracle of what he is doing in the church. The miracle of making everything new: of what he does in my life, in your life, in our lives. He builds and he rebuilds and that is precisely the reason of our hope. '

The conversation that takes place between the woman and Jesus is full of the promise of a hope re-kindled. Jesus is offering the woman a priceless gift which was a way to wholeness and deep peace. What happened to her? She felt as though she had a fountain of living water bubbling up within her that she could not contain. It was rekindled hope and therefore new life.

We too can experience that hope in the midst of our messy, broken lives. We too can have our thirst quenched and be filled again with hope in the goodness of God. There is nothing too great for God to heal and transform. There is no sin, no brokenness, no hurt, no pain that God cannot work within and bring hope again.

Just recently I had an encounter with a woman who is a recovering alcoholic. She shared her life story with me and I was so glad to listen to her as she shared. Her name was June and

she had held a very high-powered job as a senior social worker.
She described the pressure that she was under to hit targets,
manage staff and work transparently. Her career mattered more
to her than anything else and the relationship she was in suffered
and eventually broke down. Her life was spiralling out of control.
What began as a reward for a hard day's work, a glass of wine,
had taken over her life. She told me that she would keep alcohol
in her desk drawer just to get through the day. Eventually she
was discovered and sacked. She lost her home and ended up on
the streets selling herself to buy the drink her body craved.

One day she was drinking cider just behind Fortnum and Mason
in Piccadilly, London, when a former client recognised her. June
had been very good to this woman when she was in need and
the woman remembered. She took her home with her and
allowed her to stay for nearly two years until June was able to
get herself somewhere to live and maintain it. June was amazed
at her kindness and it turned her world around. She was filled
with hope that life could be different. She went along to
Alcoholics Anonymous meetings, which she said was the hardest
thing she had ever had to do. It took several years before she
managed to hand things over to a higher power. When she did,
she found a hope within her that had never left her. It was a
hope in the God she had discovered. Hope became a reality in
her as it has to in all of us.

That hope is to spill over from us into every aspect of life. Be
filled with hope for the world. Do not deny the darkness that we
see in wars and horrors. That would be foolish in the face of all

that happens in our wonderful yet fragile world. We have to acknowledge the deep brokenness that is all around us or we live in some sort of false Utopia. However, our hope is in the person of Christ and in his promise to draw all things unto himself. Ultimately all will be well. That is why we can be filled with hope in the midst of darkness.

Be filled with hope for the Church and for the future of the Church. That can be hard sometimes, but we can draw hope from the vision that Second Vatican Council gave us. This is the highest teaching authority in the Church. It presented a vision of hope in the goodness of God. That vision of hope can be found most clearly in the document *Gaudium et Spes* or *The Church in the modern world.* In it we were invited to give the world 'reasons for living and hoping'. What word of hope does the Church have to offer the world? I think it is the knowledge of unconditional love and the awareness that, because of that love, there is purpose and direction for humanity. That leads us to live in this world full of hope for the future and willing to let hope flow through us so that others can know that life is not a lottery. The world is tired of our ideas and theologies. It is tired of our religious practices that we try to force people to be part of. It will believe love. It will believe life that is given and received.

We have lived in our heads so long, just as the Scribes and the Pharisees did, that the world no longer listens to us. People vote with their feet as they struggle and search for what brings life abundantly. I was reading something recently that I found quite challenging from Richard Rohr. It was this: 'Until we Christians give evidence that there is life on this side of death, the world does not need to believe our dogmas and giant churches. It does not need our words of hell. It needs our promise of heaven'. Unless we love we have no hope to offer the world and that is essentially what the Gospel is all about.

We can live in hope for humanity. I love Matthew 25 which is the parable of the last judgement. Jesus uses typically rabbinic language to persuade, as he reminds us of the heart of his message that we have to love one another, and that the more we love, particularly the poorest of the poor the more we are loving Christ present within them. That is what gives us, and others, hope in the goodness of God and in the future promise of eternity. The Kingdom of God will only be seen in, and through, love. Ronald Rolheiser says, 'Jesus is clear, as were the great Jewish prophets, that, at a point, religion is about how we care for the poor, pure and simple. There is perhaps no more frightening text in Scripture than Jesus' teaching on the last judgement in Matthew's gospel, chapter 25. He tells that, on the last day, we will be judged by God on one basis: did we care for the poor? Did we give bread to the hungry, drink to the thirsty, clothe the naked?'

I guess we are being asked the question, 'Are we prepared to be love in the world?' 'Are we prepared to be compassion in the world?' Not for what we will get out of it simply because our hearts have been so touched by love and hope that we cannot help but reach out. Note that the virtuous did not realise they were responding to Jesus, but to the poor and needy. That is

when the Kingdom will be seen to be a reality and when people will be drawn to Christ and recognise that he is King of love and his kingdom is all about love. South African Archbishop and Nobel Peace laureate, Desmond Tutu, declares that there is always
hope when people care and are willing to take action. One of his famous quotations is this: 'Hope is being able to see that there is light despite all of the darkness.' See the hope that is all around us as people reach out to the destitute, feed the hungry and do all kinds of extraordinary work. It brings the light of hope in to the darkness.

I met Mark many years ago when he was a cynical accountant who thought life was about making money and having a good lifestyle. His marriage had fallen apart and he was struggling to find hope. He came along to a gathering that I was part of and was blown away by the welcome he received and the openness of others. He kept coming back and although at the time he would have said he had no faith, something was growing within him. He met Sue and they fell in love. They married and still he continued to come. One Pentecost, he cried out to God after feeling challenged at a meeting by someone sharing their experience of the Spirit. He now says, 'Something happened that day when I cried out'. Something did. Mark's heart was opened up and he heard the call to love. He was catapulted into the world of homelessness and drugs. His whole life is spent in caring for those who are at the bottom of the heap. He feeds the hungry. He listens to people. He campaigns for better social care. He weeps and rejoices with the addicted. He prays with them and he comforts them. Mark still comes to our gatherings. He still questions and wonders about his faith but he loves, and there are people alive today who have a little bit more hope because of Mark.

There is much to be hopeful about. Hope is at the heart of the Gospel. Take time to let the hope within you be rekindled. Give thanks for the hope that is in Christ. It is a hope which tells you that everyday is a new beginning and that, in the much-quoted words of Julian of Norwich, 'All will be well and all manner of things will be well'.

# NINE

# GIVE THANKS FOR THE
# CALL OF GOD ON YOUR LIFE

I remember many years ago, my mum decided to invite two students from the University of Liverpool to Christmas dinner. It was done with a big heart and a desire to make whoever came feel wanted in a foreign land at holiday time.

We were to be allotted students by the University. My mum wanted everything to be as perfect as it could be, a traditional English Christmas for our guests. The two students who came were polite, charming Chinese men. They ate our food, even watched the Queen which we ourselves never did but it was traditional and so had to be done on that day. We answered their questions about our traditions and also about Christianity and it was a great day. As they were leaving they asked if they could return the favour. Would we join them for a meal?

Of course we said 'yes' and, at the appointed time, arrived at their house along with my aunty Maureen who had been part of the Christmas celebration. My mum found it really difficult to cope with different food, different music and a different culture. Over and over, under her breath, my mum kept saying, 'God help me'. It was a real cry from the heart. My mum was not a bad person; in fact she was a wonderful woman of faith. Afterwards she said to me, 'I really have to change and become wider in my understanding', but on that day, for those few hours, she found it so hard.

I think the call of God on our lives is, in the power of the Spirit, be open to what I would call 'otherness'. It is an invitation to be understanding of that which is different from our own reality. Some people have said to me, 'Does that not compromise your own faith?' It seems to me that we do not have to deny our own truths to enter into dialogue with people of good will. If anything, we have to be more aware of our own Christian faith in order to welcome and embrace that which is different than we are. If we are not aware of our own faith, then we have little to share with others.

I think it is the unwillingness to love, 'that which is different' which is at the centre of much of our planet's problems. The basis of war, violence, and indeed all hatred, is the reluctance to look at another person and recognise the presence of God, regardless of their colour, creed or sexuality. At the centre of the Gospel of Christ is the mandate to love, even that which is other than we are.

Recently I was in a retreat centre with a group of religious sisters. One of them began to tell me about her ministry as a teacher in Rwanda. She told me of the children she had taught and the effect that education had on them. She spoke powerfully about the support she had received from those in the United Kingdom. Then she told me about the ethnic cleansing that had taken place in the village where she lived. She began to cry as she talked of her neighbours who had been slaughtered by others in the same village. I asked what she had done. She smiled at me and said, 'The only loving thing I could. I went and buried the dead.' This frail looking woman had gone to her Muslim neighbours and dug graves and prayed as she could. Then she buried their bodies with dignity and respect. Love, even that which is different to yourself.

If we can open ourselves to the mystery of God, we will learn to love the other and to be open to what the other brings. It is then that we can transform the world. It is the heart of what the Scriptures are inviting us into. It is the call of God on our lives and we can give thanks for the wonder and mystery that it propels us into. Mature religion is about transforming history and individuals. It is about letting the mystery of God loose in our lives so that we can learn to love otherness and not keep handing the pain on to the next generation. That is how, as Richard Rohr says, 'We can build something new, good, and forever original, while neither playing the victim nor making victims of others. We can be free conduits of grace into the world.'

In order to recognise this call of God on our lives, I would like to spend this chapter reflecting on the Beatitudes which I know I have mentioned in an earlier chapter. It has always struck me that these eight short sayings lay out Jesus' core teachings in a wonderfully intense and persuasive format. They challenge the very essence of who we are, how we live and how open we are to otherness.

You know, to follow Jesus is to allow the spirit to lead us into the process of transformation. It is in the maelstrom of transformation that we begin to hear the call to live life to the full. That necessitates living with the values of the Beatitudes at the centre of who we are. If we are going to be honest that means we have to change within and begin to see things differently and find goodness in everything. To live lives of compassion, love, mercy, forgiveness and justice is difficult. To live lives where we are always looking for goodness, and are filled with awe and wonder, is not easy. To change our understanding of who God is and who we are is not an easy journey. To see goodness everywhere, we have to change as we let go of hatred and bitterness and learn to embrace everyone.

I guess, really, what it comes down to is the death of the ego which will lead us to love what is different to ourselves without judgement or condemnation. Peacemakers, seekers of truth and justice, merciful ones will always see the presence of God in that which is different.

Most of us do not want to recognise the unpalatable truth that difference, of whatever kind, can rock our equilibrium. At times it frightens us and can sometimes bring out the worst in us. It is much easier to reject and push away that which is different than it is to welcome and embrace what is other than we are.

Yet, Ronald Rolheiser makes the point that welcoming what is other and different is a central biblical challenge. In our Christian tradition, there is a paradox that we are invited to hold and trust. It is that, while God is within us and amongst us, God is also beyond us. We are challenged to hold that balance and to know the truth that God is always more than we can imagine. When the ancient writers call God holy, they are reminding us of this truth. I am told that the Aramaic root of the word holy means 'separate' or 'cut off from'. God is holy, not because of all the strange understandings we have of holiness and piety, but because God is other than we are.

So in our Christian Scriptures we have the great tradition that revelation from God comes mostly through the stranger, the foreigner, the unexpected, the unfamiliar, in what is different, in the surprise. The Scriptures insist on the importance of welcoming strangers, strangers who, if we care to look, will reveal the presence of God to us. Look into the First Testament and the story of Abram, Sarai, the birth of Isaac and the three strangers who reveal the presence of God. Look at how often Isaiah and the prophets speak of the word of God coming through the stranger and those considered to be other: Ahaz a pagan king, Naaman a foreign general. How often does Jesus in the Gospels show the revelation of God in the life of someone who is considered other, like Samaritans and lepers and tax collectors and prostitutes? Why would I talk about otherness when about to reflect on the Beatitudes? It is because to live the Beatitudes is to live a life of open vulnerability where otherness becomes our friend, the stranger, a means to see the presence of God, the unexpected, a chance to be open to the grace of the moment. Of course all of these realities are occasions for gratitude.

So let us begin to look at the Beatitudes, with that wonderful
call to be poor in spirit. 'Blessed are the poor in spirit for theirs
is the kingdom of heaven'. The phrase 'poor in spirit' harks back
to the 'anawim' of the First Testament. They were the little ones
who knew their need of God more than anything else. They lived
with an inner attitude of receptivity and openness, as we are all
called to do. This is the only way we can possibly receive anything
from another person or situation, and so it is the only way that
we can receive from God. Yet, often, we are so full of certitudes
and self-righteousness that we are unable to be poor in spirit.
If anything we are so full, we have no room to receive. How sad
when this is the case!

There is a wonderful Zen story that illustrates this teaching. A
young man, who wants to become the student of a particular
teacher, is invited to a meeting at the master's house. This young
man begins to try and impress the teacher and goes on and on
about all his achievements. The master listens without saying a
word and then begins to pour a cup of tea. He pours until the
cup is full and then he carries on. The cup by now is overflowing.
Eventually the student notices what is going on and interrupts
his monologue to say, 'Stop pouring! The cup is full.' The
teacher's response was, 'Yes, and so are you. How can I possibly
teach you?' I wonder, have we learnt the lesson?

So we move to the second Beatitude. Matthew has Jesus say,
'Blessed are those who mourn for they will be comforted'. I think
this is hugely challenging because we are being invited to live a
life where we can enter into the pain of the world. We are to

weep for the children of Syria, to feel the pain of war-torn Yemen, to let our hearts be broken by the famines and droughts that haunt our world. Sadly most of us run away from pain. We do not want suffering, but the pain and the suffering of the world teaches us to yearn for justice where there seems to be none, to crave peace and freedom for those whose lives are shattered by violence and unrest. We are being invited to mourn for the state of the world without needing to blame or judge anyone, but instead recognising the tragic reality that both sides are usually caught up in. It makes us ask questions like, 'How open am I to the things of God? How willing am I to really enter into the pain of the world?'

The relentless invitation to a transformed life goes on as Matthew has Jesus then say, 'Blessed are the meek for they will inherit the earth.' I read somewhere that a better translation is 'Blessed are the gentle,' and perhaps an even better one is 'Blessed are the gentled.' I do not know if you have read the *The Little Prince* by Antoine de Saint-Exupéry? If you have, you will remember the passage when the prince asks the fox, 'To tame something: what does that mean?' The fox teaches him, 'It means to form bonds. If you tame me, we will need each other. You become responsible forever for what you have tamed.'

Cynthia Bourgeault who is an Episcopalian Priest says that is the area this Beatitude is working in. Blessed are the ones who have become spiritually 'domesticated': the ones who have tamed the wild animal energy within them, the passions and compulsions of our lower nature. It is a little bit like the story of the man who describes his inner life as being like two wolves fighting each other. His grandson ask his grandfather, 'which one wins' and the grandfather says, 'the one I feed.'

Bourgeault goes on to say, 'Only when we have dealt directly with our animal instincts, and the pervasive sense of fear and scarcity that emerge out of our egoic operating system, are we truly able to inherit the earth rather than destroy it.' So have you been 'gentled'? Until that process begins within you, there is not much chance of you being open to otherness.

The concept of justice is stated exactly halfway through the Beatitudes as Matthew has Jesus say, 'Blessed are those who hunger and thirst for justice: they shall have their fill.' The call to be just is repeated at the very end of the Beatitudes again. I think that to live a just life in this world is to be willing to identify with the longing and hunger of the poor, the disadvantaged, and those who are oppressed. Our identification with them always leads to conflict, even amongst those who should understand. As I have written before, when we began to feed the homeless in the Parish I lived and worked in, most of our opposition came from the daily Mass going population.

The Beatitudes then invite us into a life of mercy as Matthew reminds us when he has Jesus say, 'Blessed are the merciful, for they will receive mercy.' I was once told that the word mercy means undeserved kindness. Mercy does not come to us because of any sort of merit on our part. It is undeserved. Every I day I thank God for mercy, that free gift of undeserved kindness which is lovingly poured out and which demands nothing in return. It is a gift from the one who is always the giver, the one who never demands repayment. Mercy is simply there for the asking, and to begin to realise that brings the most extraordinary freedom. Mercy is of course to be shared. We give mercy and we receive mercy. The root of the word 'mercy' comes from the old Etruscan word 'merc', which also gives us the words 'commerce' and 'merchant.' It is all about exchange.

Cynthia Bourgeault puts it beautifully when she says, 'Usually we think of the mercy of God as a kind of divine clemency, and we pray, 'Lord have mercy upon us' as a confession of our weakness and dependency. In this other understanding, mercy is not something God has so much as it is something that God is. Exchange is the very nature of divine life - of consciousness itself, according to modern neurological science - and all things share in the divine life through participation in this dance of giving and receiving.'

Jesus seems to instinctively know this, as he shares the nature of God with those around him. We too are invited to be willing to share mercy we have received with those that we meet, even, and particularly, in the lives of those who are other than we are. Much of what we do damages the flow of mercy as we refuse to be open and welcoming and aware of God in others' lives and that is the challenge this Beatitude faces us with.

Then we hear the invitation, 'Blessed are the pure in heart, for they will see God.' It begs the question, what is purity of heart?

I guess for many people, it has to do with sex and being virtuous. It would be roughly synonymous with chastity, perhaps even with celibacy. However, I am told that in wisdom teaching, purity means singleness, and the proper translation of this Beatitude is, really, 'Blessed are those whose heart is not divided.' When Jesus was baptised in the Jordan, he had an extraordinarily powerful experience of the love of God. This experience enabled him as a human being to know that he was loved by God, which could only mean that he was fulfilled in his humanity. It is only when we know the truth of love for us that we recognise our fulfilment in Christ. Then we can only become single minded for the Gospel. I read recently that the Aramaic word to describe this is 'ihidaya', meaning the 'single one' or the person who has drawn together all the fragmentation within. This transform-ation takes place primarily within the heart. When our hearts become focused entirely on the one who has given us life or when we desire one thing only, then we will see God. So this Beatitude is about cleansing the lens of perception. It is about opening your eyes and seeing the presence of God, even in what is other or different.

The next Beatitude, 'Blessed are the peacemakers, for they will be called the children of God', follows as the rational consequence of all that has been written in this chapter. When our hearts are gentled and single, when we have tamed the wolves that fight within us, we become peacemakers. We are no longer suspicious of others motives, nor do we look for badness in others who are different than we are. We simply accept the wonder of God invading our lives. It is then that our own inner peace flows into the world. We become vessels of harmony and compassion.

Sadly most of us are not really peacemakers. We divide and separate. We set up camps of the like-minded. We reject that which is different and other and it leads to disharmony and anger and suspicion. It does not have to be like this. The Spirit is calling us to be disturbed and move beyond ourselves into a wider, more spacious, more generous way of living where we are at peace with ourselves and with the world and all who live in it. It is a huge challenge and one that we can only be grateful for as it stretches us and invites us to grow as human beings and as faith-filled people.

Most of us have a very narrow interpretation when we read 'Blessed are those who are persecuted for righteousness sake, for theirs is the kingdom of heaven.' We presume that the Beatitude is talking about martyrdom. It seems to be about receiving our eternal reward when we have been faithful in withstanding persecution. In fact this Beatitude is more about freedom. It refers to being so free within that whatever negativity is levied against you, it has no power.

I will never forget the words of John McCarthy who said of his captors, 'They can imprison my body but never my mind.' Whatever this liberation may be, it is what the journey is all about, to be so detached that whatever is thrown at us can never destroy us. That is a slow process of letting go and entrusting ourselves to God. Situations of persecution can become great teaching tools if we have the courage to use them that way.

These Beatitudes lead us into a radical transformation of consciousness. It happens through a willingness to enter into a relationship with God and it involves a commitment to domesticate those violent passions within us; and above all, a passionate desire to unify the heart. The result of this means that not only can we live with difference but we can enter into relationship with those who live and see things in a different way than we do. That is counter-cultural. In western civilisation, it seems to me that we are being invited to reject and even hate the other. Jesus is inviting us into a new way of living in a new world. The Beatitudes are the means by which the Kingdom of God, which is this new world order, comes about. They take us beyond the mere fulfilment of rules which the commandments gave, to a life-style based on vulnerability, self emptying and co-operation, where the other is valued, respected, loved and desired.

As the Sermon on the Mount goes on, Matthew has Jesus spell out practically how a person filled with spirituality of the Beatitudes would live. 'Love your enemies' must be one of the most revolutionary messages of all Jesus' teaching. Who are our enemies? In some cultures Muslims are despised for being Muslims, anti-semitism is on the increase, gay people are hated and persecuted, women are treated as second class citizens. The word 'enemy' can be defined in so many ways. Love those who hurt you. Who do you reject because of the pain they have caused you? What institutions are you suspicious of because of the negativity they have had in your life? Loving that which is different to yourself is hugely challenging.

Ronald Rolheiser, says that the willingness to love your enemy is right at the centre of the challenge of the Gospel and captured in that phrase is so much. He writes, 'This challenge is what sets Jesus' moral teaching apart from others and gives it its unique character - and its real teeth. This is meant to be the distinguishing mark of a follower of Jesus: he or she can love and forgive an enemy.' We cannot do that by ourselves. It has to be God's love flowing through us into the life of another. We need the power of God because then we can love the enemy, the hurtful, those who are different.

The Sermon on the Mount continues as it reminds us of the radical nature of following the Lord. Jesus says, 'Do not judge'. Why? I think it is because judgement destroys the human community. It stops people living life to the full. It will always reject those who think differently or see differently. Yet, who are we to judge anyone? If the call of God on our lives is to transform the world through our openness, then how can we judge any other human person? We must learn always to seek goodness and look for the presence of God. Jesus illustrates his commandment with the saying about the splinter and the plank. It is a simple fact that we do not see our own faults. When we do, we quite often transfer what we see in ourselves on to others. It takes the heat off. Dietrich Bonhoeffer in *The Cost of Discipleship* wrote, 'By judging others, we blind ourselves to our own evil and to the grace which others are just as entitled to as we are.'

A few years ago I went to listen to a Priest from South America who travels all over the world sharing with people his vision for the future of the Church. He was very interesting to listen to. At one point he said that the future of the Church does not depend on how many priests we have or whether we can get to mass. The future of the church depends on how willing believers are to get down on their knees and wash the feet of those around them, because that is where our credibility lies. Is foot washing not as much about accepting difference and living and loving otherness as it is about feeding the poor? Is it not about respecting and honouring the presence of God in every human person? Dietrich Bonhoeffer wrote, 'The renewal of the church will come from a new type of monasticism which only has in common with the old an uncompromising allegiance to the sermon on the mount. It is high time people banded together to do this.'

This call of God on our lives is hugely demanding as we have to let go of a way of thinking and being that has probably been the only way we have known. However, it is also very fulfilling as we are led to people and situations that we might never have found ourselves in. To love that which is different is radically transformative for ourselves and for others. So it is right that we should give thanks for the call of God on our lives.

# TEN

# GIVE THANKS FOR
# THE CALL TO HOLINESS

John was a larger-than-life character who lived in the south of Ireland. I met him on one of my many visits there. Sadly he is no longer with us but his influence has continued in the lives of many people he knew. John had never married and, at one point, had tried his vocation to the priesthood, but the rigours of seminary life were not for John and one day, after months of trying to fit his square peg into a round hole, he just walked out. He was not welcomed back too profusely by his family. They were ashamed that he had left and did not quite know what to do with him. His uncle had a cottage on his farm, miles from where his parents lived, and it was there that John went to stay. He was initially supposed to stay for a few months, just while he got his life back together. However, months turned into years and on into decades. The farm passed from generation to generation and 'uncle John' was just part of the fixtures and fittings. He lived a simple life, mostly alone, but he was a man of enormous wisdom. His semi-monastic way of living had enabled him to see the presence of God all around him. It was in nature and the changes in the seasons that he found God, and because of this he was an extraordinarily holy man. John's life had set him apart, the true meaning of holiness, and enabled him to see clearly. He brimmed over with good humour, peace and joy. He was an amazingly well rounded human being, and the key to it was gratitude.

He told me how for nearly sixty years, ever since he left the seminary, he had been in the practice of thanking God each morning for all that he had been given. Even when his life had been hard with the rejection of his family and his banishment to the cottage on his uncle's land, he had practiced gratitude. When there seemed no reason to thank God, John would walk for miles, and in the stuff of creation would find reasons to thank God. He told me that this practice of gratitude had spilt over into his daily life and he recognised the presence of God more and more in the ordinary experiences that he had. He said that when he left the seminary, he had been very bitter and angry but had slowly experienced freedom from bitterness and resentment as gratitude took over his life.

It reminded me of something I read many years ago by Ronald Rolheiser that I am sure I have mentioned in other books. He said that the only heart which can transform the world is the grateful heart. I think it is because, in the heart that is grateful, there is no room for the cynicism and the bitterness that has scarred so many of us. In the grateful heart there is only room for acceptance, understanding, compassion and love. It is those things that transform our broken world, and the key to it all is gratitude.

As I listened to John and spent time with him, I knew that I was listening to a holy person, and I began to realise that holiness has its source in gratitude. It has to do with the recognition that everything is gift. Nobody owes us life, a living, service, or love, and so when we receive these realities, our only proper response is to be grateful.

Sadly, we have made holiness about the religious practices that we undertake as though they were a mark of anything more than the routine of religious duties. Somebody once said to me that they doubted even Jesus and Mary would pass some of the strange tests that we think make a person holy. I think the questions that we constantly have to ask of ourselves are these: Am I becoming more grateful because of my Religious tradition? Am I becoming less bitter and cynical and resentful because of my relationship with God?

Gratitude is the key to holiness. It is the value that underpins transformation. It is the reality that will save the world. So, even if you have to do it through gritted teeth and in the face of seeming disaster, cultivate gratitude and see the effect it has on you and on those around you.

Many years ago I read the book *Prison to Praise* by Merlin Carothers and it had a profound effect on me. It is the amazing story of one man's journey into the mystery of God. It tells how he learned the power of praising and thanking God in every situation that he found himself. The more he grew in the practice of gratitude, the more aware he became of the presence of God. In the book, Merlin tells of his own very tough start in life including trying to run away from God at an early age and of the transformation he found in coming to faith and of various stages of his journey after that. These stages included him receiving what is called the 'Baptism in the Holy Spirit' and learning what he called the most powerful lesson of his life - the practice of praising God in all circumstances, even and most especially, the difficult ones.

I think our ability or not to be grateful even in the worst of circumstances is a sign of the depth of holiness in our lives. I learnt that from a wonderful woman called Therese. I met her when I was fifteen. Her life's experience had been very difficult but her encounter with God had so touched her heart that, despite her difficulties, she would never stop thanking God. She said that through a violent and failed marriage and through bringing her daughter up alone she had learnt to be grateful for the ever-present God. God had been her security and her strength. Therese's daughter had huge issues and for long periods of time would not even speak to her mum. Despite the pain, Therese would continue to thank God. She never once blamed her daughter for her actions. She learned the wisdom of compassion and forgiveness even in the face of the lies her daughter told about her. Her life of gratitude meant that I knew a very holy woman.

What do the Scriptures tell us of the power of gratitude that leads to holiness? The earliest writings in the First or Old Testament can be found in the book of Exodus where the writers tell the story of Israel's escape from the wicked hands of the Egyptian Pharaoh. When the People of Israel cross the Red Sea they are filled with gratitude to God for the freedom they have been given; so much so that they burst into song and dance led by Miriam, Moses' sister.

The book of Deuteronomy is an invitation to give thanks for the gift of life and the relationship we have with God. In the book of Chronicles we have, in chapter 15 and following, a liturgy for installing the ark in Jerusalem. It has in it a lengthy psalm of thanksgiving, which shows the spiritual climate of the celebration and includes David dancing before the Ark of God. How many of us would be free to dance in the presence of God? The reaction of David's family, who think his dancing a disgrace, shows us I think that very few of us have that sort of freedom or even commitment to God that would make us dance with delight. David is so grateful to God that he dances. Holy people are never plaster saints. David certainly was not one of them; but holy people are at times reckless in their love of, and response to, God as gratitude spills over.

In the book of Joshua, a covenant renewal takes place in Shechem, one of Israel's central sanctuaries. Following the customary form, there is a recounting of God's saving action, beginning with Abraham and the early patriarchs to Moses and the exodus, and the eventual settlement in Canaan. After the litany of the Lord's wonderful actions, the people are asked to show their gratitude. There is a huge challenge in this. How grateful are we for God's presence in our lives and does our gratitude lead us to live lives that are solely for the Lord?

In the Psalms, we find, particularly in the Psalms of thanksgiving, a real spirit of gratitude. The Psalms always reflect and recognise the truth that God's hand is at work in our lives, now and in the past. Cultivate a sense of wonder and awe. Be amazed by things. Resist becoming jaded. Let the mystery of God stir your imagination. Celebrate with all your heart. Do not lose your sense of wonder. Allow everything to teach you of the presence of God and rejoice. It will lead you to holiness.

As you reflect on the prophets, you discover that they never stop hoping, and so are always filled with gratitude even when facing the people of Israel with the mess of their lives. The Prophets will never throw out the promises of God. They believe in them wholeheartedly, and gratitude overflows from them as they hope in God their saviour. Hope is not just wishful thinking. It is believing the promise. It is an attitude towards life. It is a way of living and being in the world. It is always expanding your horizon. Many years ago I read the book *Hinds Feet on High Places.* It is the story of little Much Afraid whose transformation leads her to the high places. On her journey, Much Afraid learns that when God shuts the way ahead, you turn to the right. When the right closes down, you turn to the left. There are a lot of people who try to plan their lives wishing and hoping for a particular outcome. When nothing happens and their plans are not fulfilled, they lose hope and gratitude flies out of the window. Hope keeps us believing, keeps widening our horizons and fills us with gratitude. Isaiah, in particular, is to go and tell the people to trust and to hope in God but it is also true of Hosea, Ezekiel and Jeremiah. Hope leads to gratitude, which leads to holiness.

The most famous passage in the Gospels about gratitude has to be Luke's story of the ten lepers. Some years ago, I watched a programme about a refuge for battered women. It was very sad listening to the stories that were told, real stories of rejection and violence. The amount of pain that existed within the lives of those women was incredible. The saddest of all was an Iranian woman. She was a Muslim who had been battered and who, despite the fact that all these women were in the same position, had been rejected by the others because she was Muslim. She said that the others hardly spoke to her and that, because of what was happening in Syria and Iraq at the time, she had been set upon and beaten. It is amazing how quick we are to judge others and blame others and exclude others. We all seem to need to be part of the in-group.

In Luke's Gospel, there is no such thing as a group that are in and a group that are out. One of his favourite themes is that of inclusiveness. He wants us to know that we cannot force the kingdom into a neat, square box that has its boundaries. We cannot say that some are in and some are out. Luke reminds us over and over again that it is a waste of energy doing that because God is always bigger and more than we can imagine and acts outside the parameters that we try and put on God. The kingdom is in the love, joy and peace that exists between people. We are never going to be able to quantify it and measure it. It is within the church and it is outside it. It is shared, it is quiet, it is at work, it is powerful but it is never going to be subject to quick and easy distinction. It does not have a membership card. It is amongst people and sometimes amongst the strangest of people. One of our lecturers at college often used to say that many of us would be surprised by the people we had to sit next to in heaven.

It is almost to illustrate that truth that Jesus tells the story of the ten lepers. Lepers were considered to be unclean and were forced to live outside the community. So they represent those who were on the fringes, those who conventional society would shun or treat with caution. We have modern equivalents of lepers in our society today. I am sure that we could list them if we tried. Some of them might be people who live on the streets or those who have mental health issues. Maybe those who struggle with sexual identity and gender issues are also amongst those who could be considered, in the eyes of many, our modern day lepers. One of the lepers in the story Jesus told was a Samaritan. So he was even worse than the others in the eyes of Jewish society. Jews and Samaritans hated one another for historical reasons so not only was he an outcast but he was a hated outcast. Yet it is in him that the power of God is at work. He is the one who recognises what Jesus has done and gives thanks. He is the one who is filled with gratitude.

It is a reminder to us that God will not be bound by our petty understandings and self-righteousness, which limits the power of God and the presence of God. It is an invitation to take the risk to open our eyes and to begin to see the presence of God at work in people of all sorts of persuasions and backgrounds. It is an invitation to join the Samaritan in thanking God for all that God does in the lives of God's people. Gratitude leads to holiness, even in the life of a much-hated Samaritan.

One of my favourite writings in the Second or New Testament is the first letter from Paul to the Thessalonians. Paul concentrates on thanksgiving and gratitude in the letter. which is unusual in the body of letters that are attributed to Paul. Indeed, gratitude makes up the largest part of the letter, whereas it does not seem to take up too much room in his later writings. Maybe that is because, as theology develops and grows, there is less time to reflect on the basics. There is a perceived need to get the developments in teaching and reflection across but you do find, even in Paul's later letters, allusions to thanksgiving.

So in this letter Paul urges us to give thanks. What is it we are to give thanks for? The clue lies in the little word grace. As always, underneath everything he says, does and writes, the bottom line is grace. 'The grace of our Lord Jesus Christ'. The word grace means that which is free. God has poured out love on us freely without us having to earn it. God is pure, unmerited love. If you try to concoct any system where you think you can earn grace or achieve grace, then, as it says in the letter to the Ephesians, grace is not grace. That is hugely challenging to those of us who were brought up believing that the life of faith is a rewards system. The moment it is earned, the moment you think you are worthy of it all, then it is not grace.

I find it surprising how many people, when life deals them a rough hand, say, 'It is not fair; I have never done anything wrong.' It is as though life is somehow a series of merit points that we earn. This love that we are talking about does not operate in that way. It is a love that says, 'I know what you are like. You do not have to pretend because I love you anyway.' That truth is so freeing. Jesus is pouring that same grace on us today. All we have to do is believe and trust and allow it to flow through us. When that begins to happen, we will find, like the Thessalonians, the way to a life of gratitude and holiness. Pray constantly that you be filled with gratitude. Maybe our prayer has to be the willingness to sit and choose gratitude until we become grateful.

Maybe we have to praise God until we ourselves become an act of praise. Paul is obviously aware that one of the things that makes us different to others is whether or not we are grateful, and so he places a great deal of importance on thanksgiving.

So the Scriptures remind us that gratitude is at the centre of our lives as the people of God. Through ancient stories, reflections, prayers and songs, we are invited to be grateful and that gratitude will lead us to holiness.

One of my friends is called Pat. Pat has suffered for many years from mental health issues. There have been times in her life when she has attempted to take her own life because the pain has been so great. She has also self-harmed down the years to try and free herself from the pressure of that inner pain. She has heard voices, compelling voices, that have told her she is no good and that others would be better off without her. So hers has been a tough life, but throughout it all, Pat has never stopped believing in the goodness of God, and when her state of mental health allows it, she is filled with thanksgiving and gratitude.

When she is stable and well, Pat grabs hold of life and lives every moment. She is excited about everything and grateful that she can do it. She loves to sit and watch the world go by, thanking God for the people she sees. She marvels at the beauty of the world around her. She takes great joy in the little things of life as well as the bigger things. Her life, because it has been so hard, is precious to her and holiness shines through as she thanks God for every minute of life she has been given.

As well as in the Scriptures, gratitude has also been very much part of our Catholic Christian tradition. If you look at the writings of St Francis of Assisi, you will find that he only passed down to us prayers of praise. He lived his life finding new realities for which to praise God. Most of them were the ordinary things of life - nature, animals, the situations he found himself in, the communities he lived with. For whatever was happening in his life, he continually praised God. He seems to have had an ability to celebrate God's love in everything he saw and experienced. St. Teresa of Avila, who lived from 1515-1582, was a Spanish mystic, writer and reformer of the Carmelite order. She was an influential and pivotal figure of her generation and known as a holy woman who knew the wisdom of gratitude. She wrote, 'In all created things discern the providence and wisdom of God, and in all things give Him thanks.'

St. Gianna Beretta Molla was an Italian pediatrician born in Magenta in Italy on the 4th of October, 1922, but grew up in the Lombardy region of Italy. As a young girl, Gianna openly accepted her faith and the Catholic-Christian education she experienced. She grew up viewing life as a wonderful gift and found prayer to be hugely necessary if one is to live life to the full. She said, 'The secret of happiness is to live moment by moment, and to thank God for what He is sending us every day in His goodness.'

St Ambrose was a bishop of Milan who became one of the most influential ecclesiastical figures of the 4th century. Ambrose was one of the four, original, doctors of the church, and is now, the patron saint of Milan. He saw the value of gratitude when he said, 'No duty is more urgent than that of returning thanks.'

St. Augustine of Hippo was a Roman African. He was an early Christian theologian and philosopher from Numidia, whose writings influenced the development of Western Christianity and Western philosophy. He was the bishop of Hippo Regius in North Africa, and is viewed as one of the most important Church Fathers in Western Christianity. He, too, knew the value of gratitude when he wrote, 'O my God, let me remember with gratitude and confess to thee thy mercies toward me.' John of Avila who lived in the sixteenth century, was a Spanish priest, preacher, scholastic author, and religious mystic, who has been declared a saint and Doctor of the Church by the Catholic Church. He is called the 'Apostle of Andalusia', for his extensive ministry in that region. He understood the primacy of gratitude in difficult times when he wrote, 'A single, 'Blessed be God!' when things go wrong is of more value than a thousand acts of thanksgiving when things are to our liking.' Pope St John Paul II, too, was aware of the power of gratitude when he said 'Remember the past with gratitude. Live the present with enthusiasm. Look forward to the future with confidence.'

They, along with millions of others, have recognised that gratitude is key in our growth as Christians and that the holy person is always the grateful person. The converse is also true. The grateful person is always the holy person. So why not try and pray to have a heart full of gratitude? There is so much to be grateful for in life, but it is a hard journey to let go of negativity and be grateful. Be grateful even for the things you do not like. I guarantee it will change your life.

Some years ago I went to Russia. My primary reason for going was to visit the Hermitage museum in St Petersburg. It is in a gallery there that Rembrandt's famous picture of the Prodigal son resides. In order to get to St Petersburg, we joined a coach of Americans and Canadians and travelled via Belarus and Moscow and on to St Petersburg. The trip was full of wonderful memories like breakfast in a hotel in Belarus where an American woman asked for a second cup of coffee and was told 'No' in no uncertain terms! As we travelled across Russia, somewhere between Moscow and St Petersburg we stopped in a small village for coffee. As we were wandering around, we met a wonderful old woman. Our guide told us that she had nothing other than the shack she lived in. Why was she wonderful? It was because she was grateful for the little she had. Gratitude had touched her life, permeated her very being, and shone forth from her like a beacon.

I think that the call to gratitude is a huge challenge to us. Do you have a grateful heart for the grace that God has poured out on you? Are you grateful to be alive? Are you grateful for the gifts that surround you and that are within you? Is your glass half empty or half full? Gratitude is one of the cornerstones of the Christian life and is a pre-requisite to holiness. Why? because it sets us apart from others who do not grasp that the very reason for our existence lies in the hands of another. To be grateful is to be counter cultural. So, choose gratitude whatever may be going on in your life and let it lead you to holiness.

# CONCLUSION

A few years ago I was in the Holy Land. One day I was wandering around the old city of Jerusalem when I witnessed something extraordinary. An elderly Palestinian woman slipped on the cobbles and before I could get to her, two Jewish men had rushed to her side, lifted her to her feet, and made sure she was alright before going on their way. In a place of such polarisation between peoples and where hatred and anger are often the energies that govern much of what happens there, it was an amazing thing to witness. The woman was obviously filled with gratitude towards the two men as she thanked them profusely.

Whenever I see something like that happening, I am always reminded of Paul's letter to the Galatians in which he writes, 'There is neither Jew nor Gentile, neither slave nor free, nor is there male and female, for you are all one in Christ Jesus.' It seems to me that this is one of the basic truths of our faith yet most of us pay lip service to it. While we might not be in as polarised a situation as that of the Holy Land, we still divide and separate into good and bad and right and wrong. We still find it difficult to live with difference. Most of us fail to recognise the presence of God in those who live, think, act differently than we do and at times we are not very gracious in our attitude to those who are other than we are.

Until we learn to be grateful for all that God has given us for the life that we have and the encounters that we have, we will never be open to our brothers and sisters and we will never be able to co-operate with God in transforming this wonderful world. I hope my meanderings on the subject of gratitude have helped you on your journey in faith. I hope that in and through my faltering words, you will have heard the call in your own life to give thanks with a grateful heart.

When we celebrated Pentecost this year, my prayer was that the Spirit of God would enlighten my mind, broaden my vision and help me to be more grateful than I might otherwise be. Wherever we are on our journey in faith, maybe that could become our prayer. May gratitude fill your heart and soul and may it spill over into the lives of those you meet, bringing life and light to yourself and to others.

Further copies of this book
and other books by Fr Chris Thomas

Love is The Key
When Did we Stop Skipping?
Meta... What?
Holiness is for Everyone
Forgiveness is for Giving
Let it Begin With Me

are available from:

Goodnews Books
Upper Level
St John's Church
296 Sundon Park Road
Luton, Beds, LU3 3AL

01582 571011
www.goodnewsbooks.co.uk
orders@goodnewsbooks.co.uk